FEED ME THE SUN

ALSO BY CHRIS ABANI

Fiction

Masters of the Board (Delta, 1985)
GraceLand (FSG, 2004/Picador 2005)
Becoming Abigail (Akashic Books, 2006)
The Virgin of Flames (Penguin, 2007)
Song For Night (Akashic Books, 2007)

Poetry

Kalakuta Republic (Saqi, 2001)
Daphne's Lot (Red Hen, 2003)
Dog Woman (Red Hen, 2004)
Hands Washing Water (Copper Canyon Press, 2006)
Sanctificum (Copper Canyon Press, 2010)
There Are No Names for Red (Red Hen Press, 2010)

ACKNOWLEDGEMENTS

Thanks are due to Red Hen Press for permission to reprint the title poem from *Daphne's Lot*; to Red Hen Press for "Stations of the Cross" from *Dog Woman*; to Copper Canyon Press for "Buffalo Women" from *Hands Washing Water*; and to Copper Canyon Press for "Om", "Sacrament", "Divination", "Descent", "Processional", "Pilgrimage", "Benediction" and "Renewal" from *Sanctificum*. "There are No Names for Red", from *There are No Names for Red*, was first published in the USA by Red Hen Press.

CHRIS ABANI

FEED ME THE SUN

COLLECTED LONG POEMS

Poetry series editor: Kwame Dawes

PEEPAL TREE

First published in Great Britain in 2010
Peepal Tree Press Ltd
17 King's Avenue
Leeds LS6 1QS
UK

ISBN 13: 9781845231569

Supported by
ARTS COUNCIL
ENGLAND

CONTENTS

DAPHNE'S LOT

"The mistake they make, most of them,
is to attempt to determine and calculate,
with the finest instruments, the source
of the wound"

Harold Pinter
A note on Shakespeare

1945

When the magic mushroom clouding Hiroshima cleared
on peace, Daphne was fourteen. Her imagination could

not measure the desert of death that was Normandy's
beach or the oily cough of tanks through small dusty

Italian towns where everybody wanted to be Americano!
But she remembered waking to the siren of the air-raid

alarm, disoriented by blacked out windows.
The shelter; a family huddle under the stairs

with the musty smell and the tang of cleaning products,
face pressed into the familiar hardness of the ironing board.

There was the thrill of the gasmask and the free candy
she got at the local cinema on Saturdays if she

remembered to bring it along, and the ballerina in her
music box that lived only when she hoarded sweets.

2001

I pretend to smoke my pen, listening to Beethoven.
Moonlight Sonata. This is the thing.

Long hours, late hours, much of it tortured,
waiting for sense like patterns in the sand.

Or language poetry or conceptual art.
To say: Oh my craft and the time it is taking,

but Derek Walcott got there first and how
do you follow a poet like that?

I cannot call Mum. It is four a.m., this late,
the tone would be loud enough to touch.

I want to ask – did Granny brush your hair,
the moment fragile yet tensile as a strand of that hair?

I need the material, but this thing, this shape
cannot be found with her. Like the rabbi said,

never give up a good question for an easy answer.
And this much I know – the deeper art

is to follow where the shape leads,
but my fear needs a map. Lines, in couplets,

to contain the uncertainty. Still it mocks me.
Oh my craft, and the time it is taking!

1937

There had not always been the war, unfettered
weed in the garden of Europe, over-running neat

boundaries, like the bed Grampy tended and grew
the flower Mum would be named after.

There had not always been the austerity shrinking
joy to a half remembered child's song or unwilling

parlour games shadowed by boredom. Daphne remembers
village fetes with prize pumpkins, cakes, pies, needlepoint,

dancing displays, of which she was part, tombola stalls,
coconut shies, darts and sandwiches in untidy piles.

2001

There are memories we carry forgotten
only to stumble over them suddenly,

like the lost fingering of a B Blues scale;
flooding visceral, and whole as the ball we bounced

off heat-wet tarmac, ghosts at the edge of night.
Daphne had forgotten she was the only girl to pass

the eleven plus exam in 1942, even as Hitler opened
up the Russian front. She turned down the scholarship

to grammar school, choosing the secretarial.
And though she tries, the regret is heavy in her voice,

like the smell of mangoes
rotting – sweet, so sweet.

What was the fascination with the black metal
machines built by Remington that fired sixty words

per minute in the hands of a pro? The labour-heavy
way the ink carved the page? The oily smell

calling to a time when scribes mixed lampblack
with bitumen and blood, before crafting themselves

into myths old even then? Or perhaps it was
the impulse filling her diaries, defined in her evenings.

*

Henry John Hunt. There it was like the proper edges
of the desk he sat behind in the fading photograph,

pen held rakishly, the smile daring the camera to fill
the white page. Staining the yellowing back: *Dad. 1925.*

Grampy left school at twelve, though he loved
the classics and paintings – *The Blue Boy* in particular.

Apprenticed to a bothy, his passion, for colour,
transferred to flowers and shrubs. Daphne's

notes don't say why he left school so early
and why he chose gardening.

"Mum. It's me. About Grampy. Did you know why?"
Static depersonalises the distance, yet I clearly hear

her sip hot tea before: "I don't know, Chris.
Those were different times. Is it important?"

My silence is the rolling of the phone
between moist palms like an udara seed.

"No, Mum." Finally. "I love you, bye."
Rushed. My discomfort shuffling

the photos that will not lie,
and yet will not reveal my family to me.

1948

The funk of barley from the Horlicks plant,
the grey of this town not even winter's rain could wash.

Escaping the mechanics of prediction, Daphne did not
hit the factory floor but became the youngest

secretary to the boss, though she shared the same
canteen as the workers in blue – so old they were

like a washed-out sky. The bleakness of the room
broken by the tired sun floating in the grimy window.

Gladys, who worked the night shift, saw the grey reflection
in Daphne's eyes. Wrestling with much reluctance

the cigarette from her mouth, she said through smoke rings:
"Get out, lass. While you still have your looks, and can."

1950 – 1953

How small town girls dare. This may not be a recipe.
Refuse the scholarship others will die for.

Work for the boss of the local factory.
Leave that lucrative position, off the factory floor.

Become an au pair to a South African couple.
Move to Maidenhead; shock everyone.

Single girls do not leave home. Leave the South
Africans when the children grow. Move to Taunton.

More shock. Bristle like a sharp pencil behind
the polished oak reception desk of an hotel, a hotel.

Come home on weekends to a family that treats you like
a celebrity. Asking questions. Awe. More questions.

Until the television arrived. Then no more
questions. No more celebrity. Each return followed

by: *Shush, not now honey; Coronation Street is on
the box*. She hated that ghostly black and white tube.

Other things required for the dare. Drink. Dance.
Laugh. Leave Taunton and move to Oxford.

Find employment as a secretary during the day;
at night, party or go to the theatre club. And sit

opposite your future husband. But by all means
be oblivious. Do not notice him.

1954

In the sleepy cold academia of Oxford that had
more bicycles than China, she became his reason.

He found excuses to visit the College office –
applications to the glee club that could not be trusted

to the postman. Essays for his postgraduate in Geography –
handed in early. She pretended not to see him.

Though the horns on her spectacle frames seemed perkier.
Finally, he asked. "I'd be delighted," she replied.

The cafe probably had a name like Joe's or Harry's –
an avant-garde cappuccino bar. In black and chrome,

it held the participatory promise of beatnik-Kerouac-
Jazz-poems, and always, the steam of coffee.

When they met on a winter's eve for that first date,
Mum felt, as she drank in the dark coffee

of his skin, that she was turning. The mist on
her glasses softening him into the man she hoped for.

*

Then the party later, and the American rock and roll
that seemed made for the easy looseness of his waist;

eliciting envious glances from stiffer dancers,
whose practised movements had been charted

across dorm-worn carpets, with the precision of calculus.
The subtle gyration of his hips as they danced held out

the promise. Later he walked her home across
a gravel-crunching path hemmed by grass sequined

in dew and light. Was it his easy laugh, the way his
hand brushed her elbow – present yet not too familiar?

It grew as she whispered to her friends at night;
warm as the hug of shoulder-wrapped blankets.

*

And what songs did they claim with the novel optimism,
and though Dad maintained their relationship was chaste,

Mum's shaded smile spoke deep. When did they cross
the imaginary line drawn by parents, and the convention

of society in the fragility of eggshells, whose crack
hatched passion sweatier than a jungle malaise?

*

"Tell me everything."
Outside, the rain was the landscape,

here in Devon, at the tearoom beside the sea.
On the table, the revolving tray, an island

on the ocean of white, was laden with sweet treasures.
His hands, like black gulls or the grumbling

of clouds before a storm, fluttered between the craft;
cups, saucers, sugar bowl and milk jug. Each teaspoon

an oar. He sighed. Reaching for a scone
he broke it open on his plate, divining crumbs

for the point of origin, buying time,
knife dipping, graceful as a heron fishing,

into the clotted cream before spreading the truth,
cemented with jam. The back of his throat burned

with the need of words not spoken, selected
with care from among the hot coals of his thinking

like slow roasting yams. There was the savannah
that rolled into a long ochrous dry pant; trees

so alive they seemed to wear their leaves rudely;
or the birds flaunting colours in the thick of green,

paws-paws so ripe their weight was a torture,
and yet the trees wept sap with each plucking;

the ululating song-call of women working,
or washing cassava roots in the river,

voices pulling your heart into your tears.
"I want to know your deepest secret."

Tea, gulped too fast, too hot, burnt past the crush
of words, releasing: "My mother is mad."

Daphne's poised cup, the pause of her shock
came down with a clatter and spill. Then

her hand covered his gently. "And I am afraid."
Her silence, open, un-asking, like the gaze

of a newborn, was the thing that would
become her life with him.

*

Her parents had not met any black men until
Michael's purple-black sheen and easy smile.

Grampy said it reminded him of that other black
fella with the trumpet. And Granny – little eth –

heating and reheating the spread 'cause
"They like hot food," until the tea was sharp enough

to cut and cucumber sandwiches
peeled away, like pages curled from use.

1957

Mum boarded the rickety propeller plane bound
for Enugu. Skeletal, like a sunburnt dragonfly,

it seemed held up more by hope than science.
Unsure what to pack, her cases were swollen

from the uncertainty. Books. New sheets. Crockery.
Cutlery. Records. Slacks. Shorts. Blankets. Tea. Coffee.

Cheese in tins. A wedding dress. A little loose, in case.
Armed with only Dad's exaggerations about how

primitive it was. Bush everywhere and potentially hostile
natives, like a scene from a Cecil DeMille movie.

She was pleasantly surprised to see Whites milling
everywhere, stores that sold Robertson's marmalade

and vanilla ice-cream on crumbly biscuit cones.
Houses. Cars. Roads. No cannibals or wild animals.

And Dad, with his brother and cousin, their haircut
sporting a middle parting known locally as "I don't care",

waiting next to a shiny new car that sat on
the tarmac's edge, its top humped like a polished

tortoise shell, curving away like a spyglass reflecting
all the possibilities around. The heat, like a fever

sweated out, forced from her pores, the illusions
about this land birthed in Europe's imagination.

And it was not a dark continent. If anything,
it was too bright for her new sunglasses, horn-

rimmed like her others. Was she disappointed?
After all, danger was half the adventure, half the romance.

And that first journey inland, sticking to the plastic
seats. Did she take anything in? Or was she concentrating

too hard on being attentive to the endless welcoming
yammer of the men, while trying not to be sick

from the unevenness of the road, the heat and the cloying
smell of melting hair pomades and petrol. Her stomach heaving

with every sway of the spring dashboard-mounted grip
of the statue of the Holy Virgin of Fatima. Like many

of the bad memories of Nigeria, she cannot remember.
But there would be challenges ahead, rougher perhaps

than the drive. She bore them all with a stoic resignation
that would have made any missionary proud.

The village was closer to the frame of her imagined
picture. No electricity; mud huts and sand flies

that feasted on her fresh, plump, pink flesh.
She lived in Ogbeka's house, roofed in shiny corrugated

iron for her arrival, chaperoned until the wedding
in the local Catholic church after her conversion

from the Church of England. The ride from the church
in the borrowed Land Rover, though bumpy,

was not long enough. Settling in quickly, endearing herself
on her first morning by frying plantains and eggs

for Michael's breakfast, over an open wood hearth.
Grand Uncle Idume Chukwu, priest, shaman, seer,

bone-setter, figure as mysterious in family folklore
as Melchizedeck, studied her silently with a wry smile

as though his shaman spells had lured her here, to this land.
Her place in Afikpo's Hall of Fame was quickly cemented

when she had three sons, born in rapid succession,
confirming her husband's virility.

That and the smattering of the native language spoken
in a painful accent, clear that she, the white one, venerated,

was humble, was all these honest people needed.
Dad fought his mother's derision for Daphne –

calling her the pale wraith, with skin cold and pink
and goosed like a pig's or plucked chicken. Her blue eyes,

shadowless like a vengeful spirit. Not a doctor or nun like
the other whites on Mission Hill. No car like Mr. Brown,

the district commissioner. Dances like an epileptic.
Cannot haggle in markets or tell how long to smoke

fish or meat, or which leaf makes a good soup,
which a poison. With hair like *mami-wata*,

useless for farm work as the sun would burn her
to crisp, like overdone *suya* – her mother-in-law

ranted, listing Daphne's faults. And Dad smiled
indulgently, translating: She really likes you.

Says you have translucent eyes; hair like a goddess.
She thinks you are heaven-sent. And Daphne's

smiles rotted her mother-in-law's guts, as
nothing she said about her seemed to cut.

What became of it? In what unremembered season
did it begin to unravel like a wick left untrimmed,

stuttering its flame, hiccupping shadows?
Was there a time when the exploration and conquest

of her body's mystery, inhaled along with steamy sea
smells, was a madness for him? The warmth

had receded into slow dying embers, left too long
unattended by passion, and we were witness to ashes.

By the time I was born, it had worn to a habit.
Flared to passion only by pain, and then it was just fighting.

*

And for Michael? First graduate from his town,
whose father had been a houseboy to the Irish priests

who recognized Michael's promise with a scholarship
to the University of Cork. Then Oxford. Did the burden

of the town's hope weigh heavier than rain-drenched
firewood that burnt with reluctant and rebellious smoke?

In a town so self-involved that marriage outside
was discouraged, what did they make of Daphne, really?

What pressures did he suffer silently until that silence
sat in his throat, a rough seed of resentment?

Did he feel he had to prove himself unchanged by it?
The strength of his intellect, bent, honed itself

to a cruel edge. Not sure how to be what he never was
he perverted the lie until it was a barren river bed gloating

at his own fear. Like Achebe's Okonkwo, his bravado undid
him, stitching a shroud too tight to do anything but unravel.

And did he ever explore his inner skin, safe like
an umbrella's shelter, or did he, like me, shy away,

believing, as he was told, that touching the inner skin
of an umbrella causes it to leak, the rain overwhelming?

1962

In those early days she kept diaries recording
in cursive script: Dawn treading blueberry

and orange footprints across the sky. Night rolling
the sun into its pocket, like a child's forgotten yo-yo.

Streams crossed by bridges of slippery tree trunks.
The kiln-like heat. The sun, yawning shadows across

the sand, melting the distant river into thick sluggish
chocolate. Air plants clawing sheer rock, ephemeral

as the sculpting wind, held by tenacious hope.
The river, where black swans dipped their heads

in regal acceptance of the fishes' adoration.
Dust roads, winding like terracotta slashes against

the greenery. The silence of pre-dawn settling like
a casual blanket draped against the cold.

The single vulture-beaked tap in the yard,
where the clash of metal buckets sounded like swords

drawn to honour, as women carved a space to breath.
Dried, ready-to-harvest rice, swaying.

Stars at night, struggling against the deeper
darkness, like fireflies defying street lights.

Then changing mood with the abruptness of a needle
scratching across vinyl, lines describing heat,

rashing the skin between her legs – red, burning
in the salty sting of sweat. Then the deeper secret.

Gathering like dark clouds preparing to break, the sun
hidden, it brewed thick like tea with too much tannin,

good only for curing buffalo hide. Then the fists unleash
the storm, tattooing her body in bruises like marble cake.

The violence always there. Then skimmed over,
for the children's sake. But that did not negate

the lie of her heart. She still loved him.
Then pages returned to the crackle of termites boring

thatch, drying clothes yawning in a cat-stretch across the line.
Her diaries held it together until the weight was too much.

Maybe the Greeks have a point when they say:
Love is in a pile of shit, be careful you don't fall in.

1966

When the troubles began, my family lived in Igboagu,
where locals were gifted in decapitation with farm

implements; the quarrel always over land.
Whose. Yours. Mine. Theirs. Identity.

Loading the springs of station wagon low,
my parents and older siblings fled to the relative safety

of Afikpo. A fishing town on the way to nowhere.
Period. Dead end. No strategic importance

to federal troops, they reasoned. There, in their newly
constructed one-storey villa, nestled between Mgbom

hills, optimistically named Rainbow Valley, they prepared
to wait out the war. Sweat it out like a bad fever

caught in the trapped heat of blankets and Vicks Vapour Rub.
Life, unhurried as ever, made its way through, despite raids

from planes too high to target effectively. Like errant
eggs from a basket, or nest, the weight of bombs bent

the air into an arc as they fell on surrounding bush
and farmland. The tremors travelled through the earth

to nestle in the navel. And everyone, face down, felt
the incredible awe of it, composing prayers like

a deaf Beethoven scripting orchestral manoeuvres
from the vibrations. The salt-taste of tears, the body's

betrayal. Muffled sobs, ill-disguised desire –
like the itch of a match which is fire.

Finally the jets depart, peeling back sky, heat searing
it closed again. Standing, voices called melody first.

Then words. Spontaneous. Yet approximating ritual,
so we are not washed away by the deeper meaning.

Watching, on the sidelines of the astral plane, and deciding
this was too much fun to miss, I pushed bloodily

into the war, screams on lips in December, clipping
Christmas by two days, a slight miscalculation.

My labour was Mum's longest, her hardest. Doctors said
my big head almost killed her. Shamanic grand Uncle

says I will need it for my life's work. Head butting
the competition? Mum says it was a natural omen

of an inflated ego to come. One writers need
to define, redefine, limit, expand, create, challenge

in the face of deity. Annoyed that my sleep was disturbed
by noisy bombs, I cried endlessly, until Mum, pregnant

with Stella, stooped for me or asked my eldest brother,
Mark, to carry me. Face worn into a frown from my weight,

his ten-year-old muscles strained against the harbinger
of my current three hundred pounds. Later in Lisbon

he lugged me around till tears of tiredness, pulled
by the burden of this responsibility biting into childish

shoulders, ran freely. But no good griot gets ahead.
The tale has rules. Hard. Fast. Structured. Beginning,

middle, end. But like Jazz, room always for the gifted
to improvise, create, digress, circumbobulate.

2001

The Biafran flag's half-risen sun was like a mind
not quite made up. Fluttering from a bamboo

mast roped to the side of a balcony, it is the sail
of our hope. Rays bleeding out, eleven of them,

spines that would curve into questions: Who are we?
What, tomorrow? Unlike the twelve tribes of Israel,

an uneven sum of our refusal to conform,
the eleven were meant to represent the still

unnamed provinces of Biafra. Or so the book
said. Maybe they were: The eleven principles behind

the new nation. Or the eleven reasons we were
fighting for our survival. After the exhibition

in the Tate Modern, in London, I hoped
the eleven rays had been fingers pointing to peace,

like the eleven stones which Michio Horikawa
sent to the world leaders in nineteen sixty-nine.

1968

When high-flying bombers came round, again, Dad
decided it best we spent the day at Mission Hill,

Edda, with Father Frayne. Packing enough food
for the day, we waited while he went to evacuate

the Red Cross station, its bright red flag, a clear target.
Mum also packed important papers, photographs,

what memories we could take, irreplaceable,
or too precious to lose. Promising to return in fifteen,

Dad left. Even as his Peugeot cut a smoky path,
federal troops landed on the beachhead at Ndibe,

three miles away. The stranglehold had begun.
Hilary, Dad's cousin, just back from America,

was fly-fishing, his hook teasing currents, flirting
with fish, seeking a bigger prize, a certainty

not possible in that snake of muddy-gold, sloughing
old skin every second, never the same river

twice. He saw the heavy booted assembly;
cutting through back roads, he arrived

breathless. "We have to leave now," he panted.
Mum was adamant in waiting for Dad.

"Well I am taking my brothers," he retorted,
herding the older boys. As they left, Mark grabbed

a bag of food and Greg, Charles the storm lantern
that would prove so valuable. Seeing her children

trudge up Mgbom Hill, and knowing she could
not be separated, Mum, eight months pregnant,

strapped me on her back, scooped up her memories,
and pursued. Two miles later, Dad caught up

and we rode in comfort, past long lines of refugees;
the asphalt, long dark river, winding down to hopelessness.

In Edda that night, high up, we watched as our town
was torched, the militia resistance routed

with a few crackled shots – the Biafran army long gone.
Our warriors had learnt from the British that a cutlass

and a brave heart are short work for bullets.
Father Frayne, breathless from his gargantuan tummy,

helped us put up cots in Catholic school classrooms.
The integrity of the priest's house, bougainvillea

mortaring its brick, holding up walls, its purple stain
shocking the whitewash, could not be compromised

by female presences, even in war.
Three days later, troops in soldier-ant columns tracked

up the hill and we moved to Nguzu.
Those who stayed behind with Father Frayne and God

were massacred in the Church, the priest forced
to watch, as helpless as his tears. In Nguzu,

Dad's friend, a fellow member of parliament
in the first Republic, gave up his bedroom for us,

sleeping on mats with others. Hearing the gunfire
from nearby Edda, and occasionally a scream,

I imagine Mum slept uneasy, waking often at the rustle
of death's robes, as geckos trapped our dreams on mud walls

that crumbled under their claws. In whispered prayers,
in the spaces between rosary beads, she seared God's heart,

bending fear to hope. Then. On the move
again, route carefully mapped by Dad.

We separated from Granddad and other family.
There were no tears or hugs. Just tight handshakes,

casual mind-how-you-go's and gruff grunts.
But it was all there in the eyes. They circled back,

cautiously using old hunting and animal trails,
a skill long forgotten before this war.

We moved on – Edda – Nguzu – Emekuku – Mbaise,
the landscape changing as fast as our circumstances.

Sometimes as night stole through a haze of rain
we would stumble into a deserted village,

silence hanging over everything, like
the echo of a scream. The only sign of life –

hens meditating under a tamarind tree.
Huts, wearing beehives of thatch, walls cored where

bullets had stuck rude fingers into the mud.
From the car window, a field of corn rowed the plain.

All along the savannah, intermittent shrubs nailed
down the carpet of unruly grass. As we drove,

the clay of swamp roads, cooked in the heat of day,
cracked into fine tendrils, mapping our progress,

unravelling our future on the earth's palm.
And the trees lining our flight, heavy with shadows,

foreboding, like the insistence of a storm's dark
lashing, kept us from sleep's easy. And its absence,

rather than marking the passage, blurred instead,
all of our tomorrows into one unsated sigh;

a sweet longing for release. Nights were hardest –
lampblack, the primal stain of nightmares.

Parked underneath some trees at the roadside,
the surrounding forest let out its breath in a solo

mosquito whine, the bark of wild dogs, the eerie laugh
of distant hyenas, or the rope saw of a big cat.

Night eyes adjusted, filtering dark into grey
shadows. In a tree above, a monkey coughed,

irritated by the harsh smoke of a cigarette, sucked
on by a skinny stranger shivering to the left.

Vines wound around trees, leafy boughs wrapping
the moon up tightly. Then, just as quickly, dawn ripped

night's fabric, stars falling as dew, and we would be off
again, past deserted sidewalks, scratching themselves

with dry leaves. Through abandoned villages, where mud
walls, crumbling in the sun, seemed caught in the moment

before a sneeze. A pot of half-boiled rice, curdled starch
on a dying hearth. A door stood open, an exclamation.

A bicycle lay in a heap, its back wheel still
spinning. A full length mirror, leaning outside a hut,

wearing an elaborate carved frame of cherubs,
was mottled where the quicksilver had eroded,

furring like fungi across a lake. There were markets
where baskets spilt their contents self-consciously

in the sand: a montage of plantains, oranges and melons.
The clenched fist-dome of the mosque, sieved by bullets,

let in dust, like salt to a shaker. The dead Imam clutched
a fistful of prayer beads, some still pinched between

forefinger and thumb where he must have worried them,
the wood re-grained in sweat. Once, Greg thought

he saw ghost soldiers walking among corpses, eyes
cast down, backs bent by the weight of rain and sorrow.

Sometimes we had to leave the road, driving across grass
plains extending like a crinkly sunburnt blanket,

or the crust of a cold shepherd's pie.
Tall iroko and silk cotton trees scratched

the sky at regular intervals, some wearing a yuletide
spirit in their green leaves and the snow of their white

feathery boles, hanging from top branches like cotton
torn from clouds. Others, nude, gnarled in silvery dance,

dared our imagination. Paw-paw trees signed
the fading sun with five-fingered leaves. The sun,

in response, flared a few times, then bled to night,
on the knife-edge of the horizon. Despite

the ever present death, hunger and gunfire,
the African landscape continued to unfold.

Mornings with the honest fresh smell of dew-damp
earth – like innocence in the heat of lust, it was lost

in the afternoon. Lightning sliced the plumpness
of the hot sky, heavy with moisture. Thrown

by invisible warriors, rain speared the earth, each point
bleeding mud. Death was cloaked by the heat devils

puddling the black tarmac. There were also the cravings
for things we had never had, dredged up by the subconscious

from magazines and TV, tormenting
with the impossibility of it all.

Perhaps the greater craving was for life, sweeter
even than the cold vanilla of baobab fruits .

*

Years after the war, Mum discovered Sister Twomey,
her obstetrician, had confided in Dad that after my birth

and its complications, she would not survive childbirth
outside of a properly equipped hospital.

His original plan had been to have Catholic missionaries
shelter us, if the town fell in his absence, to quarter

us with the Sisters of Mercy. We never kept that pact.
Later we heard troops ransacked Mission Hill

looking for hidden Biafrans, holding frightened nuns
at gun point, while discussing the appropriate actions

to take. Finally, as a deterrent, they shot Sister Carmalita.
Dad's route never took us within thirty miles of a hospital

at any time. Moving ahead of invading troops,
we finally arrived at Mbaise.

To get there we drove through besieged Owerri,
a circuitous route intended to avoid capture

by federal troops hovering like dragonflies skirting
the edge of a pool. In the bombed skeleton

of the cathedral, its dome an open O! puzzling the sky,
steel girders raking the ephemerality of clouds,

sombre novenas for peace were said by a priest
and a congregation rapidly losing faith

in the grand design. In the debris-strewn courtyard,
the wind, tracing rapidly replaced patterns,

demanded oracular truth from the indifferent dust.
In that refugee camp in Mbaise, missionaries

catered for the strays of war. One stood out
in the postwar tales, grief plaited carefully

into cornrows that tidied jet-black hair into an order
missing from her life. So young at seven,

yet her sorrow was deeper and blacker than the dry
well where her mother was shot scraping for water.

The other kids teased her constantly. But she never
spoke, or fought back. When asked why, she said:

Dead people have nothing to say.
A few miles away, Emekuku held the only hospital

still working. Dad left Mum at least two gallons
of petrol hidden under fragrant ahunji, smell disguised.

If he could not be there for Stella's birth, he wanted
to be sure she could buy a ride to the hospital.

*

Mum's waters broke and joined the invisible salt-
stain of other births, a little over a month after

we fled Afikpo. Emekuku was still relatively
untouched by war, but Stella screamed

into the world already fighting for her life.
The staff wanted Mum to stay overnight,

but she insisted on getting back to her other
children in the refugee camp before anything

happened. Though only a breath away,
the staff at Emekuku believed the accounts of war

were exaggerated and when it entered the town
months later, under heavy artillery fire, the hospital

had no evacuation plan. The death toll, heavy.
It is true; miracles find you in humble places.

*

Captured when Enugu fell, Father Desmond's arms
were broken wings, like an angel of the first fall.

They healed crookedly. Mildly put, like *the tea*
has run out, he says, "I was tortured."

Dressed in a white soutane, he explained his mission.
There is only one God, and Allah is his name.

"Mercenary!" the Hausa officer accused,
not confused by Desmond's Dublin accent.

Missionary. Mercenary. All the same,
if you helped Biafrans. Taken back to Lagos

over many days, interrogations, beatings,
he was released with orders to leave posthaste.

As the order omitted Biafra, Desmond tried to slip
back behind advancing troops.

He was rearrested and given a one way trip to Dublin.
Weeks later, healed, Desmond pulled all strings,

bent double under the limbo line. He was not alone
in this. Many returned. "It is the children you see."

*

Night, along with whine of mosquitoes, brought safety
from Nigerian bombers, whose Egyptian pilots

would not fly in the dark. Someone's opaque logic
hired pilots from a nation who lost a war in six days.

But here we grasp at straws. The deal is always,
take it, or leave it. Yet even in day's bright glare,

refugees haunt road fringes, shaded by palm trees,
too tired to run from these gifted pilots

who come in too high to avoid anti-aircraft fire.
These attacks are a respite from the daily trudge

up and down roads, dodging the enemy
in a chess game that shuffles ever forward

and backward, territories as ephemeral
as the hope of surviving intact.

*

State House, the grandiloquent title was too heavy
for the miserly tin shed that was Uli airstrip's

waiting room, Biafra's brave face on it. Customs
and immigration formalities pretend this besieged

fledgling into being even as it shrinks from the size
of Ireland to a postage stamp eighty miles across.

At night, the generator thumps lights, when there is diesel.
Otherwise the runway lights, oil lanterns, flicker in the rain,

but never extinguish totally. Even God is not that cruel.
Flights, irregular as constipated priests who, on first arrival

ate only bread, not trusting the unfamiliarity
of yams, are held up by torrential rains,

or overexcited anti-aircraft fire driven by bored troops
taking out flocks of night birds for bets.

The Holy Ghost fathers run this widened highway
sometimes called "The Sidewalk," – or, more intimately,

Annabelle, by pilots who swear she seduces,
thinking of it as nectar nestling between the fringe

of trees – female. Occasionally a tepid crate of beer
comes through and the Holy Ghost fathers

drink till they break into Irish sea shanties
that would make a stevedore blush.

Pilots, passports stamped with the old capital's legend,
jibe Biafran officers about being lost, as Annabelle

is one hundred miles west – the joke funnier
because of the Igbo officers' humourless looks,

all spit and polish in torn, much-patched uniforms
stiff with starch of sweat, and Wellington boots

polished to a sheen with palm-oil, their gleam
marred by tiny insects attracted to the sweet oil –

sticking, they bubbled the rubber into a rash.
The war flies in the face of it,

belying all odds, held up by
a ragtag army and drunken priests.

*

We waited in Uli, nearest village to Annabelle,
the widened highway Biafra's last working airstrip,

for three nights for a plane headed back to Europe.
As day's embers died into night, we would leave

the untidy spread of the town – houses scattered
like broken pottery, roads running like spilt water –

for the airstrip. The soldiers guarding the gate were gaunt,
their eyes reflecting the hopelessness of it.

War is a self-perpetuating state.
After a while, it's about nothing but its own sake.

In the corner, in the shadows, another
family crouched silently, wearing the darkness

like a skin. Night after, gathered in the little
hot zinc shack serving as an airport lounge,

we counted moths slamming to death on the thick
glass of paraffin lanterns. Games Mum played

to distract us from the sounds of encroaching gunfire
and the boredom of the wait. Patiently we watched

planes come and go, followed by Mark's and Charles'
questions. Why not that one, Mum? I imagine she

smiled resignedly in the face of the constant pestering.
We cannot take a plane that stops overnight

at São Tomé. Because they don't let Biafrans
stay overnight, sweetie. Because the Portuguese

government won't let us. Because the Nigerians
will bomb it. Aren't we Nigerians? We used to be,

but now we are Biafrans. Hush now!
Sometimes we sat outside; it was cooler around

the fire that twitched sparks into the dark. We waited,
reunited with Father Frayne, our breath caught

in a choke as we heard big guns approach.
Finally a plane limped in, slicing a gash

in the jungle. It would leave in an hour
and we could go on one condition.

We had to fly on the outbound plane from São Tomé,
which had a burst tyre with a temporary patch.

It was a risk less frightening than the approaching
death. The question hung in the air, pregnant.

Father Frayne nodded. Mum, confident of the priest's
power, consented. We landed in São Tomé, island

off the coast of Gabon, in time for breakfast.
Our stomachs, fisted in hunger, could not cope

with fried bacon, eggs, sausage. So French
mercenaries offered chocolate and smiles,

as the Lisbon plane refuelled. Mum was extra edgy
as we touched their guns. Hours before in Uli,

she almost lost Mark and Charles to Biafran guns.
My memory, cut and framed from stories,

(no doubt fuelled by romance) is as follows:
the Catholic Relief Agency plane unloaded food,

clothes, medicines and bibles. We began to board,
escorted by the Portuguese crew, frail old

missionaries and desolate Catholic priests and nuns.
The infamous Boys Brigade, Biafra's child army,

stopped us for a final search, to steal what valuables
they could. Ranging eight to fifteen, they bristled

with old rusty rifles, Dane guns, cutlasses and clubs.
Expert fingers sorted, divorcing nuns from Christ, stealing

gold wedding bands; priests lost glasses, watches,
Biafran pounds, worthless but better than nothing.

Mum had only papers, her bag of memories, the clothes
we stood in, and us. In disgust, they reached for Mark.

At ten, they argued, he could fight. To prove their point
they threw a rifle at him. Reflex, he caught it.

"See? Expert soldier," the insolent teenage commander
said. Mum pulled herself up, staring down his rifle barrel

and declared in loud voice, "I am taking him. He is
my son." Her voice did not shake, blue eyes flinty.

My mother, who panics when a teacup is broken
from a matching set, staring down death. Finally

the pimply-faced commander conceded. But Mark
only gave up the heft of the rifle with a fight,

pulled by some invisible connection to these child
warriors. Mum insists differently. I prefer my version.

The dying sun spread a purple wine-stain across
the evening sky as afternoon fluttered and died.

Just before we left, everything was still.
As night gathered its skirt, we took off,

cabin lights dimmed, treetops rustling fuselage
as we flew low, avoiding radar. The captain warned

us we would fly in darkness over Nigerian waters,
reassuring us that any turbulence was "only anti-aircraft fire".

Through dark windows, fireworks, tennis balls
of phosphorescence exploded, too beautiful

to be tracers from the guns below. Mum and Father Frayne
got the only two seats, the rest of us huddled on the floor.

Cargo planes have few seats or safety belts;
no stewardesses with sickly smiles to stanch fears

of crashing, to belie the fact no one believes several
tons of metal will fly, except by *deus ex machina*.

I remember thinking that if we were hit, we would
be devoured by sea-circling sharks wearing

a lace of multicoloured jelly fish. But I could not have.
I was 18 months old. We reached Lisbon twelve hours

later with no further incident, except when
Charles, teeth locked in terror around the rim of glass

of water, took a bite and swallowed.
The piece of glass was never found.

1968

Standing next to a breathless Frayne, his stomach
the envy of any Sumo, we realized the Church

sent no-one to meet us at Lisbon airport;
busy, foreign. Frayne commandeered a taxi

to the nearest convent, where the nuns sniffingly
paid the fare. Leaving after a hearty lunch,

he caught a plane onto London. From Heathrow
he called Gran before flying on to Liverpool.

We had to wait; six seats on standby at peak
of tourist season is a bit of a stretch.

Arrangements hurriedly made meant we had to spend
the night in the convent, leaving for a Catholic lay

pension at dawn. There in that city of hope,
under the watchful eye of the pale, plaster Christ

on the Cross, arms held high by realistic rivets, blood
rusting down gaunt body, we ate dinner with the nuns.

High ceilings, bare stone floor (Mum recalls mosaic),
and austere furnishings, wrapped us in a hush

penetrated only by nostril-tickling incense,
the solemn reading of scripture, rustling garments

discreetly adjusted, masked coughs, the warm bead-roll
of rosaries and the apology of cutlery.

It was no place for five noisy children and a tired mother,
but they coped. They spoke no English and we

did not understand their haughty, elegant Portuguese.
French, badly spoken on both sides, filled the silence.

*

At the Catholic pension, run by members of the lay
order, we found others ousted by Biafra's war.

All the expenses were paid by the convent.
Accompanied by the other refugees, we toured

Lisbon, with the convent's gift of dollars.
Lisbon, in silhouette, is Portugal's nose.

The inlet for the River Tagus opens
into a lagoon spanned by the Ponte Salazar.

Modelled after the Golden Gate, it was built
in nineteen sixty-six, in anticipation of my visit,

no doubt. Christ, 92 feet tall, arms spread in benediction,
guards the river from the South Bank, every bit

as impressive as its proto, the Cristo Redentor
in Rio. Trams haul up steep hills. Torre de Belem

noses inquisitively into the Tagus, the starting point
of many journeys of discovery, like a giant discarded boot,

its wearer crossing the Atlantic to fall off the edge
of the world. Adorned with rope carved from stone,

open balconies, shield-shaped battlements and Moorish-
style towers, it floats like a ship riding the waves

of Portugal's faith. Like curious cranes,
cannons peep out of gun ports – mouths open in pant –

its vaulted dungeon, pretending the airs
of a Cathedral. Inside the Esufa Fria, gardens

of the Parque Eduardo VII, a nymph hanging
from a mushroomed stump of fountain flirted with us,

her stomach full, rotund buttocks perched on
a disgruntled fish. In the Jardim Agricola Tropical,

the city sweated its exotic past in the gardens.
High pillars like ornately carved ivory tusks held

up the domed ceiling in the nave of Santa Maria de Belem
in the Jeronimos monastery, built in the Manueline style

by João de Castilho. Museums overflowed with bounty
from former colonies – China, India, Japan, South Africa.

Even an ivory salt cellar, adorned with Portuguese
knights, a sixteenth century gift from Africa's Benin

empire. Our pension was in the poorer quarter
of Alfama, where cobbled streets cut narrow ravines

between crumbling stone buildings. Snaking alleys held cafes,
street performers, many of whom were from exotic places,

echoing the diversity of the past. Also vendors of scabbard fish.
Eel-like, these were stacked like silver high-tension cables.

The walls of our room, adorned with tiles,
charted Portugal's past glories in faded blue.

We stood on the restored battlements of Castelo
Sao Jorge and squinted in the sun, searching

for our pension. Below us, flowers, shrubs and lawns
mapped the public gardens like the abstract designs

of Islamic-Moorish tiles that dared hint at Allah's
form in the complexity of floral and geometric

patterns spiralling and twirling into formlessness.
A stone woman, shrouded from head to toe, prayed

by the tomb of Carlos I, the concrete fall of her
garments so real I believed I heard her sobbing.

A fishing net of cable-car power lines threw itself
at the facade of the Se, the city's cathedral.

The Tagus swept up steps wide as an amphitheatre,
held up by two stone pillars, like sacrificial posts

for the Kraken, up to the palace square,
into Praca de Comercio. Mark kept the postcard

of Eça de Queiros' statue, the great novelist,
inspired by a near naked muse whose lush breasts

haunted many adolescent wet dreams. Years later
I stole it and hoarded it with other treasures,

like the soap that held my first pubic hair.
The vaulted arcades of the cloisters

of Mosterio des Jeronimos threw cool shadows
where we ate our picnic lunch with Janet and Winston,

a Jamaican couple from the hotel, ex ex-pats
of Biafra. Mum tried to feed Stella from malnourished

breasts that held mostly air. Smiling wearily she
turned to Janet and said: "I am not a good cow am I?"

Like a child's Lego model, the Aquedento des
Aguas Livers, the aqueduct of the water of life,

spanned the Alcantara valley, northwest of the city.
The monument to the Discoveries, shaped like

a caravel, sailed the square. Marching up stone sides,
huge statues of Vasco Da Gama, Pedro Alvares Cabral,

Fernao Magalhas, poets, writers, all led by Henry
the Navigator, holding a model of a cavarel.

Land-bound, the only waters he navigated
were the shark-infested oceans of finance, court

and church. It was he who bank-rolled all
the important expeditions. Spread like a collage-map

at its base, the huge stone compass donated
by South Africa held discoveries from the past,

while pointing to the future. This small, now poor,
country once colonized much of the world; then lost it all –

like spices thrown overboard, ships drowning
in angry seas. In this city, founded by Odysseus returning

to Troy, and named Ulisipo, there was so much
of us bound up in the stones, meeting, now,

on the cross of many intertwined destinies.
Passers-by gawked at the white woman

in baggy faded maternity gown and flip-flops.
One black child tied to her back, three in tow.

Mark, ragged, wore a scowl from the strain of me.
Charles and Greg followed, trying not to trip

over the umbrella. Faded flowers traced
the faint patterns which washed out nightly,

as she laundered our only clothes. Hanging
on the balcony, they dried in warm sea breezes,

oozing the stink of war. Wrapped in cool clean
sheets, we watched stars seed the night.

*

Sunday. Lunch. Mum, in her only dress, sleeveless,
came down to eat. But the door was barred

by the thin-lipped proprietress, stern face
pulled back by a tight bun, head shaking,

finger wagging every word –
"No bare arms in dining room on Sunday."

Stumped, and with nothing else to wear, Mum shrugged.
Tugged by her commitment to save the poor,

the dragon lent Mum a shawl. Taken all in stride,
stoically. After Biafra, this was easy.

Six days we tramped and trammed through Lisbon,
merry as any tourists, waiting for a flight with six seats.

When it finally arrived, I imagine Mum was reluctant
to face the uncertainty of London,

but the telegram sent to Gran sealed it.
Having nothing to pack, we left the hotel early

and waited in the airport, bored, listless but quiet.
Children soon learn that in war silence saves lives.

Keen eyes assessed us. Computing simple arithmetic
and yet wrestling with her Englishness,

the woman in the airport on her way home
with her family after a summer on the Algarve

finally strolled over: "Don't mean to be rude,
but you look like you're in some sort of trouble, luv."

Eyes scoped, sizing, filing. "I'm fine, really. I just left Biafra."
Though Britain supported Nigeria officially, the BBC

still managed to convey the terror and suffering
of the Biafrans. Moved beyond words, this stranger

offered Mum her pram, stroller, clothes, toys, anything,
everything. Grateful, Mum refused, sure that Gran

would meet us with what we needed. The woman insisted
she would wait with us at other end, until someone met us.

Mum thanked her, trembling on the verge of tears
because the horror never overwhelms you –

only the random acts of kindness. True to her word,
she waited – husband and restless children leashed

in by dirty looks – for us to come through
British Immigration and Customs, fashionably late.

1968

"I am sorry but you cannot be admitted."
The man was young, maybe twenty, his nose turned

up at the sight of a white English woman with five
black children dressed in rags. "But I am British…"

"But your passport has expired. You see?" he pointed,
ever so condescendingly. We had an international travel

document from the Red Cross. Stained, creased
and much-folded. Pinching it between fingertips, like a roach,

he sniffed, unwrapping it gingerly, "mmhming" as he read.
Folding it, fingers as delicate as an origami artist,

he handed it back with Mum's passport, expression blank,
fish-eyes dead. "Ah well, but it is not a British passport, is it?"

"But they let us into Portugal without any trouble."
"Yes, Madam. But that was Portugal." Sniffing again.

"This is Britain." Trembling, Mum exploded: "Why you…"
But he was unmoved, even by this wild woman.

"The trouble is you are travelling from Biafra. Wrong side."
His supervisor, drawn by the scene and the shouts

of an impatient queue, hastened over. Glancing
quickly at our documents and noting our sorry state,

he seemed appalled by the younger man's attitude.
We were ushered into England with deep apologies

and offers to our carry nonexistent luggage.
We emerged to find Gran and a friend.

While all around, practised,
the English stared with averted eyes.

*

Refugees in a small rural English village always make
the town newspaper, especially when a local gal,

Daphne, returns with five nigger-babies, from a war in Africa.
The thrill of gossip confused by the compassion

for her suffering and "God knows those poor children
are innocent, still that's what you get when you

go off to live in the jungle like one of them."
But many came bearing gifts in response

to the article. Clothes, toys, books, food.
They delivered all day, wearing that embarrassed

smile of the English when caught in an act
of spontaneous kindness.

*

Milngavie, a suburb of Glasgow, was as cold
as Biafra was hot, and far from its troubles.

Yet news of children and other innocents'
suffering had penetrated even here, carried

by Scottish ex-Biafran missionaries,
returned from it, but tormented that they could,

should, ought to do more. An old family friend
gave a talk to a Church women's group in Milngavie,

having asked Mum if she could cite us
as an example of people dispossessed.

Moved, they sent Christmas gifts of jumpers, hats,
knitted themselves, no doubt before warm fires,

arthritic fingers aching. Mrs. Bentley continued to send gifts
until she died years later. This is all I know of this woman.

*

We fed on steak and kidney pie, fish and chips,
crisps and Spam sandwiches, waiting out the war

in a sleepy English village suffused
with the summer-drone of eager bees,

and the brambly tumble of ripe gooseberries
at the garden's end where fairies roosted in my

dreams, while Mum in her deck-chair read
and reread the very occasional letter from Dad

that filtered through the war. There, buried among
a catalogue of troop movements, the details

of casualties, among descriptions of exaggerated
heroics and grotesque deaths, technical descriptions

of scientific advances made possible by the war –
like cars powered by sugarcane fuel, homemade

landmines nicknamed Ojukwu kettles, medical
miracles, the invention of the cholera vaccine

by Professor Njokubi, an Igbo, among propaganda
sound-bites – FREE BIAFRA, SUNRISE

ON A DREAM, OJUKWU WIN THE WAR –
is the line or two betraying his deep

yet embarrassed love. "I miss you.
Things are not the same without you."

1969

The rain, though soft, was persistent, and Mum
wanted to get us home. Biafran bodies,

not fully acclimatized, were vulnerable
to colds. We were paused by a woman's call;

she wanted to apologize, she said, for teaching
her son to be a racist. Confused but polite,

Mum wondered how this concerned her.
"Oh, it's simple really," the woman assured.

Her son had told her they had a Biafran in class,
a boy named Greg. We do, her son insisted

in the face of his mother's rebuttal.
The teacher said to be nice to him as his dad

is lost in the jungle. How can that be?
She had probed. Is he black? Pondering, her son

replied, "I'm not sure. I'll check tomorrow."
Her confession, however, changes nothing.

This was the England of Enoch Powell
and the threat of rivers of blood. All around –

each act reducing the impact of good people –
racists jeered at Mum as she pushed Stella

in a pram through the village, forcing her
off the pavement and into the road.

Chants of *Nigger-lover. Gollywog babies.*
If you want a Nigger for a neighbour, vote Labour.

Countered bravely by Mark's: *Disembowel Enoch*
Powell. But it was all around us.

Enoch Powell displaced Superman
as the popular hero in the playground

where white children goose-stepped past the blacks.
And though on the news it said Slough and Burnham

endorsed Powell's position by a majority,
when no-one was looking, they pressed

lollipops into my hand, ruffling
my kinky hair while smiling sadly at Mum.

*

Mum told me about the war I was too young
to remember, her stories, spells to banish any

lurking trauma souring the soup of my subconscious.
Night licked the last of day from the sky,

like a black and white photo turned inside out.
Gleaming stars, like teeth, over-salted the dark,

drawing out animals, whose rustles were dreaded
more because we were blind.

Ogbeka, ear tuned carefully, sifted expertly,
silently. Then his machete sectioned

a startled python into choice cuts.
Mum had refused to eat snake but conceded

to fried snails, high in iron. "I hated
their taste, like darkness. Thick, muddy."

*

Tea cooled with night, Daphne rested, feet up
at the end of a hard day's work, as the Beatles said.

A tentative moon watched through the frosting
of the window, leaning on a streetlamp for balance.

She worked as a domestic to earn money
for us to go to museums and buy books.

Puffing tentatively on the spoon handle, she stirred.
"Your lot asleep?" Gran asks, from the kitchen.

Daphne's Lot had become shorthand for us.
As though we were an albatross around her neck.

Like Lot's wife dissolving, the salt of tears
reached her lips. Upstairs, we slept.

1970

There are colour photographs of Greg and I dressed
in cowboy outfits, guns drawn against Indians

neither wanted to play. Of us on holiday
in Eastbourne, in a caravan with every modern

convenience, racing go-carts and riding tandem
bikes or splashing in rock pools.

Stella's ruffled blue swimsuit contrasted
with her dark skin, so she looked like an exotic fruit.

We ate rice and stew with chicken, waving away
annoying summer wasps from spilt lemonade.

Mum's promise of raspberry ripple
made the spicy food edible. Children in Biafra,

swollen from kwashiorkor, died crying for a mouthful
of the rice my careless foot scattered.

While Mum worried about cavities from toffees,
in Biafra, shrapnel, bullets, knives, snakes

and the ever-present hunger tormented mothers.
In Wales, we stayed in a farmhouse, crowded

in with another family. Warm, from too many
people levered into a too-small space, we kept

the terror at bay. Milked cows, rode tractors,
played farmer. Yet in a smudged black

and white photo, framed against a white wall
I breathe easier. A loner even then.

1971

Hardly able to contain herself, Mum applied
to return as the uneasy peace settled

like stiff thatch seeking comfort. Paid for by the UN
Council for Refugees, our tickets arrived

in record time. Five, with no memory of this
other home, my trepidation wet the bed nightly.

All I knew of Africa was a medallion –
a giraffe crowding thatched huts and a palm tree –

that Mum wore on a gold chain. Gran and Mum's
late night whispers, which I overheard, fuelled my fear

of an unknown dad. But Mum's determination surged
ahead of the telegram with our arrival details.

*

Lagos airport. There were no flights inland, so we
waited in the stuffy, hot box of a lounge

with no seats, filled with tepid water or hot
Coca-Cola that left you thirsting more,

while Mum was interrogated for being a Biafran
sympathizer. They had her name on a list.

Photocopies of newspaper articles,
grainy black and whites of horn-rimmed glasses-

wearing geek. A real threat to Nigeria's might.
Protests were countered by threats of deportation

without her children. Bills finally changed hands
to grant access and secure seats on a "full" plane,

which was half-empty when we boarded. At Enugu,
the capital of the defunct Biafran Republic,

soldiers with guns and scowls darkened the afternoon.
Once again, the Roman Church saved us

as Dad was not among the expectant crowd.
An Irish priest recognized Mum from before the war

and insisted we ride with him to the Diocese
HQ at Abakaliki, at least for one night,

he argued, while they sent ahead to Afikpo
for Dad. Postwar roads were unsafe and there was still

too much hunger holding too many guns out there.
Tired, resigned, Mum agreed, hiding her disappointment

under a film of dust. After dinner, Father Casey
distracted Stella and me with magic tricks.

Later Mum came to bed and I dreamt her tears
fell tenderly over me like the gossamer gauze

of a mosquito net. She could sense that something
was wrong. Dad's absence from the airport shielded

some terrible truth. With no facts, she imagined the worst.
Until dawn brought light rainfall and Dad.

Surprised, flustered, torn, not expecting us.
We bundled into his cranky, hot Peugeot,

for the long and silent drive to the village,
and I, car-sick so frequently, Dad snapped:

"This is Africa, toughen up!"
I never knew how, but Mum discovered

that the elaborate charade had been to protect her
from meeting Dad's war mistress and daughter.

But Rosemary, my half-sister,
would prove to be only one of many.

*

Daphne's diary spun a wish too precious to speak.
I want a man who smiles when he talks about me.

Smiles because he knows all of me and loves all
of me and does not want me to change any of me.

I want a man like that. A man whose voice
is the pressure on my hips when he calls

my name. Whose shallow breathing traces
the arousal of my nipples as I cook him dinner.

Whose laugh dips between my legs, catching
me by surprise and rocking. Whose hands

are rough when he touches my face honestly.
Whose embrace is desperate as though

I were the only thing keeping him from drowning.
Whose lips are moist with desire when he kisses me

and whose eyes dance with a dangerous fire.
I want, I want, I want a man like that.

*

2 by 6. The short column wears the tiara title,
Thank you from Nigeria, in the *Maidenhead*

Advertiser, December 10, nineteen seventy-one.
It states that Mrs. Bromley of the WRVS

received a letter from Dad, thanking her
and the organization for their help during

that difficult time. "May I express my sincere
appreciation and thanks for all the great help you gave

my family. They are now settled happily
in my village…," the extract reads. I used

to imagine Dad wrote it in artistic copperplate,
but it is not his style. No doubt his secretary

typed it, his only contribution the dictation
and signature, the flourish worthy of Picasso.

But it does not matter to Mrs. Bromley who said:
"This letter gave me as much pleasure as any I have

ever received." No doubt shared with gathered cronies
over biscuits, and too-milky weak tea.

*

Photographs never lie. Black and white. Time,
events, frozen. Souls straining to escape confines

of white borders. Our return to Amaizu, Afikpo.
It is all there, perfectly preserved in Mum's

red leatherette album with Greek deities
fading in gold trim. I do not remember it.

The welcome home ceremony. Makeshift palm-frond
shelters shielding sun and clouds, a field of wildebeest

grazing the sky. Mounds of food, drummers, dancers,
fading into kicked-up dust. Fused in the shade

of our new mud bungalow, I lurked sulkily,
tickled by the sun filtering through holes

in the thatch. But I do remember that everyone
spoke of the war in the present tense.

Okoh, my ten-year-old cousin and I shared
a class, Elementary One. We sat under

a Gmelina tree, makeshift desk and chairs made
from cement blocks for our new classrooms,

dodging bird shit from bright yellow weavers,
whose chattering almost drowned out the teacher.

A backfiring car had Okoh diving for cover,
shit splattering his khaki shorts.

The teacher laughed uncontrollably as we stared
in confusion. Frothing, Okoh picked up a stone

and did not stop hitting her, until her face pulped
bloodily. Crying, I ran home and told. Later Okoh

was caught up a tree. Bound, he was whipped until
he bled, voice so cracked his screams were strangled hisses.

This was the war. Grandfather told me even
the vultures fled at the depth of horror it brought.

He spat in the face of demons as he spoke,
because, he said, a land without vultures is barren;

the people cursed. Ghosts of horrors unseen,
unknown, pressed in as night spilt oily ink, palpable.

Burrowing deep under blankets, my mornings
broke in cold dried sweat and pimply itching heat-rashes.

Once, our football fell into a banana patch,
rolling into a helmet discarded by a dead

soldier. Ebere ran out wearing it, waving
a rusty rifle in one hand, the ball in the other,

and the slogan on the helmet screamed: SAVE ME
OH GOD. The war was all around us.

We stayed after school and played in the burnt-out
shells of armoured cars, careful not to startle sleeping

vipers. Or we collected shiny bullets
from the prairie where Okere, the gateman,

said a big battle had been fought. We ran,
our screams warning ghosts of our presence.

Silently they lifted off in the purity of white cattle
egrets, fluorescent beetles in beaks. The heavy chink

of bullets, weighting pockets, reassured.
Careful, after Dike lost all his fingers when

the bullets in his hand exploded in the heat,
cracking like oil-bean pods, scattering his fingers wide.

The prairie ended abruptly in an orchard
next to a stream, where bamboos drooped like mermaids

washing their hair. Whispered rumours of Hausas
burying an entire village there forbid us to play,

the fruits taboo. Defiant, we stole oranges,
running squealing and laughing to the safety

of the Anglican chapel, confident no spectre
could cross its threshold. There on rough wooden pews,

beneath ceilings sagging under the weight of bats,
we bit into the sweetness of stolen sin.

Gorged, we slept until the squeaking bats left the roof
in a cloud at dusk. In the afternoon heat too intense

for lizards to bask, when rocks dreamt of river beds
and adults slept wisely, we approached the orchard.

Hanging from our favourite tree, twisting, at the end
of a bright blue lappa, was a body.

Our screams woke everyone, and parents lectured us
on Eden and forbidden fruit. The water-weight

of death, falling through the body to swell the feet,
pulled the plumpness of the branch into a curve.

When the body was cut, the branch, with hardly
a sigh, unbent the arc, righting itself.

Dad, irate like an old testament prophet
damning some unfortunate Biblical king,

was angry that the man survived the war
by killing his own children, when the federal

soldiers pressed cold metal to his skull.
The stench of shame was thick in the heat.

1972

For years my father's temper and his tales about being
a commando in the war were more threat than story.

They held me trapped in a crippling fear that allowed
no room for self exploration. Only the desperate

need for his approval. He wore warrior marks,
several livid scars. One in particular, on his hand,

whispered daredevil bravery in its deep purple-black
smoothness. Ravenous for glory, haunted by legends

of our lineage's lore, dragon-slayers and headhunters
at every turn, he could not accept his role.

Red Cross official in charge of distributing food
and medicines, the task had been more formidable

and dangerous than fighting on the front lines
where the only responsibility was to one's self.

He further undertook the risky work of reuniting
lost children and parents, requiring a dedication,

commitment and bravery equal to any marine.
But it was not enough. So he constructed vague

accounts of valour as Captain in the BOFF, Biafra's
own SEALS, reinforcing this by terrorizing his family

with threats, sometimes fists, vainglory unravelling
in night sweats. Though Mum told me he got the scars

in a drunken brawl with Ogbeka years before the war,
the fear remained until that afternoon, discovered

under a tree where I hid, smoking a menthol cigarette,
nostrils burning from manhood, nicotine

and the suppurating mangoes littering its base;
his angry shouts were chased by his thrown fist.

It hung between us, a metaphor of his loss,
suspended in my firm grip, as he frothed and kicked.

Calm, detached, I saw only the frustrated
anger of a toddler with a broken toy.

*

Ogbeka was nicknamed years before the war.
Like Karate, his name meant empty-handed.

Back then he fixed bicycles, his skills as dubious
as the scavenged materials he used. He was partial

to chopping customers who withheld payment
with a sharp, double-edged machete. And when the police

asked for the weapon, his standard answer:
I was empty-handed. Stout arms, and legs held

up by a pot belly that belied the strength of fingers
like bear traps. Eyes, bloodshot from drink.

When he grabbed us, his knuckle rubbing our heads
affectionately, it felt like pineapples were scalping us.

I always asked. *Did you fight in the war? No*,
he replied. *My warrior years are past*. But

he told Stella and me that he had helped Biafra's war
effort by killing Hausa soldiers on the sly. Why?

With a cruel glint he replied, "To eat them, of course" –
explaining which herbs soften tough Hausa meat.

His favourite part, the fingers, spiced, fried. We were
never sure if it was a joke, but it was our nightmare for years.

2001

The message on the machine is in my father's
voice: "Chris, this is Greg. The old man died

yesterday. Early a.m. Shit." I play it again and again
with fingers stubbing hands that look like his,

yet pretend a more gentle craft, pulled with the oar
of my pen. My tears, instantaneous, surprise me

as much as the thought that I would never be a man
he could respect – like he respected the honest

way Mark held his liquor or contained the world
in meaningful science, or Charles' competitive

edge and the way he held his own in fights.
Even Greg's challenge was preferable to this son

who believed in words and love and spirits.
The question is, how do you love a man who held

his over your head, just out of reach? And though
I am grown, I realize my heart yearns for him like a child.

To glove my hand safe in his, which is strong and hard
as the cricket bat I handled expertly, hitting my anger

in the red ball, yelling Howzaat! I call my sister.
Unbelieving, she says: "I don't even know why I am crying."

In response to questions about my voice, I reply
"No, I do not have the flu. I lost my father."

As though he was misplaced along with my keys
or the wallet my mum gave me when I became

a man at sixteen and which I promised never to lose
but did shortly after. Let me count the ways in which

my father loved me: with fists drawing blood,
and real threats to rearrange my brain permanently,

or to beat the monkeys out of me. With a meanness
that would make me a man or at least angry

enough to hate the world. He loved me in my
first book-burning because, he said, you should

be studying, not writing. And when that book
won me, at sixteen, the second place in an important

national book award, he said: "If you were any good,
you would be first." In these ways my father loved me.

Yet I learned my inner shape in these ways too.
That honesty, at least outside of monogamy,

is the highest virtue and that my word is
my name and that is my emblem like an ornate

coat of arms pressed into the hot melt of wax,
sealing character. That success is good deferred.

He taught me the shame and embarrassment
of demonstrating my love, so that now when I say

nice things to friends, I fight tears of effort.
And here, in this book he intrudes in spite of my efforts

to keep him out. It would be easy with a key stroke
to erase him, but so much depends on the things

that cannot be replaced; like a red wheelbarrow,
or rain or white chickens, and is at the heart of it.

And as I peruse photos of the funeral that my politics
barred me from, exiled from my grief, I realize

that I have never touched my father's face.
My fingers smudge the sheen of the photo;

his face collapsed in on itself. Skin desiccated
from the formaldehyde blooding his veins now.

Aunt Felicia tells me they could not get his shoes on,
as though all the water in him fell to his feet.

Not for the forgiveness that I begged of him
in that dream, where he drove off in a yellow Volkswagen,

face turned away. Not for the ice-cream he bought
us as children, melted in with tiny red ants by the time

he got home, and which we had to wake and eat
in the flicker of lamps because we had no fridge.

Not for the words that I would have sold my
soul to hear him say: "I love you,"

did I return, or call, or write to say: "I love you."
The only time we hung out, on the veranda,

where we sat shelling peanuts and watching the sun set,
he said: "Find God for yourself, but make sure

that he is true, lusty, rude and alive." In that memory
I realize my deeper love – my muse is dead.

1973

Emeka, an older cousin, did not survive
the war, in spite of his mother's witchcraft.

He stares back from a photo with a cocky smile
as he leans on a motorcycle like a young black

James Dean. His mother's magic employed a tortoise
shell stuffed with herbs and incantations, armour that hung

protectively over his heart making him bullet proof.
He did not die from the bullet that tore through it,

punching cleanly out of his back. It was the shards
of tortoise shell that shredded his heart like salad

cabbage. His mother still asks everyone:
Would you follow a dog to cat faeces?

Before you can speak, she answers her own riddle:
You cannot hide the sun with your finger.

*

The "No victor, no vanquished," speech of Gowon's
at the war's end never washed with us Igbos,

his promise of acceptance, sugar masking
vile malaria pills of our childhood. Depleted

by war, primed, ready to forgive if not forget,
resume our lives, rebuild, accept the political

construct: One Nigeria. Allowed no time
to grieve, heal, we reintegrated, playing down the cost

of human suffering in the interest of peace,
our pain as translucent as a jellyfish trapped

in the sun-bright shallows of a rock pool.
A bitter pill, but we scrunched up. Anything

was better than the humiliation of hunger
and a leader who abandoned us for a life

of luxury in a neighbouring country, his name taboo.
Never spoken. All photographs burned. Become ghost.

Though co-conspirators in silence, we were not trusted.
Freed of corporeality, Ojukwu's spectre haunted

Gowon, in the face of every Igbo. So we grew up
in the hard shadow of howitzers aimed at our homes

from military garrisons in every Igbo town, peopled
by federal soldiers on twenty-four hour alert to shoot

and destroy any whisper of rebellion still left,
flitting from baobab to baobab in silver moonlight.

Eight years they watched us while making our girls
soldiers' whores, shaming our men with beatings at regular

checkpoints, imposing random curfews, flexing their muscles.
Every morning, the call to prayer cracked the skin

of sleep. Sluggish, but then as the muezzin's voice ruffled
its feathers, the call rose to a single point.

As night shuttered down like the flower we call touch
and die, Mum read in the soft glow of storm lanterns:

They are changing the guards at Buckingham
Palace, Christopher Robin went down with Alice.

*

There were heroes too. Christopher Okigbo, torn
between art and the clamour of war, cried, Havoc!

and let slip his ravaged soul, profaning anger,
till Klepkany at the crossroads called home

the prodigal, to Mother Idoto. The surviving
handful of poems immortalize his genius,

grieving this griot cut dead. Others. Wole Soyinka,
Yoruba in a war of ethnicity, pleaded with Gowon,

at great risk, to end it. Starvation. Genocide.
This spelt death not only for the Igbo, he argued,

but for our collective humanity. Three years
in solitary confinement, *Shuttle in a Crypt*,

to silence his dissent. His trial was much publicized
by a starving press forbidden to report the war.

Life in Lagos went on as usual, far from
the maddening crowd. Wole is a symbol,

the possibility. But there are those, like my father,
who grudge his conscience; a publicity stunt.

*

Believing a man must never walk head bowed,
three years later, there was no sign of the hunger

and loss of war in Igboland. Self-reliant, communal
effort rebuilt schools, homes, markets. Telephones

hummed harmony to electric pylons, army
of titans marching through jungle, and running

water coughed rust from dry pipes. Igbos returned
to the North, repaired shops, lives, trade; uneasy

cohabitation, shamed friendships, fathers who
murdered sons for marrying *nyamiri,*

and daughters who tainted wombs with Igbo seed.
In once empty towns, people scurried like red ants

over a lump of sugar. Even the burnt-out planes,
guarding the highway formerly known as Annabelle,

were gone, their metal re-crafted into utensils.
Forgotten. Vanished. Until next time. We too marked

the new. Dad's Peugeot 404, white, lines like
a fifties rocket, with the sign painted on the back

bumper that warned: *Left hand turning, no hand*
signals. And our kerosene powered fridge,

with its mirror for checking the flame that flirted
in blue and orange. And music. The Supremes

called *Baby, baby, where did our love go?*
James Brown screamed, *It's a Man's World* as Aretha

demanded *R-E-S-P-E-C-T*.
Highlife King Celestine Ukwu, the philosopher,

dispensed wisdom and dialectic materialism
to a heady beat. Then, unexpected, but much publicized,

in September, Paul and Linda McCartney arrived
in Lagos to record ***Band on the run*** at EMI Nigeria.

The record never made it into the local charts despite
Gowon's threats to radio stations. But the photographs did,

in the *Daily Renaissance* and *Sunday Times*:
Paul and Linda, like Jesus and Mary Magdalene,

wearing expressions of orgasmic-compassion,
arms outstretched in benediction to street urchins

who stared in confusion at the camera, wondering
why these white people were touching them.

But their mouths, were sealed by the precautionary
conspiracy of sticky toffees handed out earlier.

1975

At night, Greg and I snuck to Iyi Obasi, God's stream.
Lying on the wooden bridge we fished by moonlight,

smoking forbidden cigarettes as we watched the stars
gravel across the water's mirror. Occasionally a fish

would come up and swallow one. Further downstream,
in the swamp, where the river spilt mud over its bank

in an iodine stain, mangroves skated the water on elegant
fingers. In distant beer-parlours, arguments raged,

spilt with the licorice of palm-wine. Why did we lose?
We came so close. One hundred miles from Dodan Barracks

and Gowon. Ojukwu did a deal. Sold us out.
No, Nzeogwu. No, the cowardly Yorubas. No,

the Americans. They never helped us. And Lyndon Johnson
is quoted: "We cannot afford a Japan in Africa."

Always the barb lay elsewhere, for we are the great innocent.
My view? We ran out of steam. You can go only so far

on an empty stomach, empty breach, empty rhetoric.
It is all good. We are healing, picking gingerly

at scabs, their itch a fresh madness. All these years gone,
yet under the surface wounds fester. The peace,

uneasy as a whale on tarmac. We negotiate thorny
issues, religious riots, flaring up a hatred, old and fetid,

lacking only the focus of a dedicated leader.
Nation only in geography. Demanding

equality, but tipping the scales secretly.
To us, equipoise is mine, and a little of yours.

2001

I still have a bullet, found as a child and carried
for luck, a warning worn smooth by worry. That bullet,

dimpling my trouser pocket is our only hope
for peace. Its heft is the measure of a yard too long.

Atonement for lives lost too young, the sacrifice
gone wrong. Optimistically we chance to arrive

there, the horizon of tomorrow. There
will always be quarrels. Biblical in proportion,

older than Eden, siblings fight. I cannot settle
that. I can only write a poem. But I know God

still speaks to us. His spirit, mischievous as a child,
employs the daily objects of our lives. Hair curling

a comb's teeth on a sink, reflecting the falling
that is our life. Esoteric patterns branded in tea

and coffee cups, washed clean by the bleach of our will.
No Elijah or old testament prophet – unlike my friend

Musa, I have not the beard for it. Nor that selfless
love of the world and others that grains itself

in the spread of our smiles. But the compass I found
meditating under a tree on that mountain

in Los Angeles is proof enough that I have
been blessed with the path through

STONE WOMAN

Such is the power of the image:
It heals only those who know what it is.
For everyone else, it is an illness.

– Roberto Calasso

Were I to recount the vile acts committed here,
the exterminations, the massacres, the cruelties,
the violence and sinfulness against God and the King of Spain,
I would write a very big book, but this will have to wait
for another time, God willing.

– Bartolome De Las Casas, *The Devastation of the Indies: A Brief Account*.

THE WAY OF THE CROSS

The way of the Cross is a devotion to the Sacred Passion, in which we accompany, in spirit, our Blessed Lord in His sorrowful journey from the house of Pilate to Calvary, and recall to mind, with sorrow and love, all that took place from the time when he was condemned to death to His being laid in the tomb. There are fourteen Stations, or places, in the Way of the Cross, at which something took place. At each Station we should say the Our Father and the Hail Mary with love and sorrow for our sins, meditating on the suffering of our Lord represented to us at the Station.

Indulgences

Those who may devoutly make the Stations of the Cross, may gain a plenary indulgence.

Those who are lawfully hindered from making the Stations of the Cross, may gain the same indulgence if they read and meditate on the Passion and Death of our Lord for at least one half-hour.

Indulgences in accord with the new "Euchiridion Indulgentiarum", from *The Way of the Cross by Saint Alphonsus Liguori.* Catholic Book Publishing Co., N.Y.

STATION I

Jesus is Condemned to Death

V: We adore you, O Christ, and we bless you
R: Because by Your holy Cross, You have redeemed the world.

Consider how Jesus was unjustly condemned by Pilate to die on the Cross.

My Jesus it was not Pilate, no, it was my sins that condemned You to die.

De Las Casas' Aria – A Funk in D Minor

I

We had to invent a hate for it.
There is no way to decapitate a child tenderly,
No etiquette on how to feed a man
To dogs hungry with their master's denial.

We made of it a place to live, a castle,
But there is a black flower that grows
In a field of green, and for all its emerald blaze
All you see is the coal of that flower.

Though we pretend they are not human
Our damnation is the plague that we have become,
Hearts blacker than that field of flowers
And we have only this.

II

And though you confront the mystery
Between altar lights and the weight of beads
And though you mea culpa all night
The thing that it is

Will not be wished away
Nor the vertigo.
And it is not what it reveals to you
It is the thing hid

And this is the wisdom of simple things
Like a spoon, a bowl, a hoe
And the heavy fall of fruit.

*

At the Cross her station keeping,
Stood the mournful mother weeping,
Close to Jesus to the last.

STATION II

Jesus Carries his Cross

V: We adore you, O Christ, and we bless you
R: Because by Your holy Cross, You have redeemed the world.

Consider how Jesus, in making this journey with the cross on His shoulders, thought of us.

My Beloved Jesus, I embrace all the tribulations You have destined for me until death.

The Book of Generations

I

Cimatl and Tenepal begat
Malinali
Cimatl passed on to the great darkness
and Tenepal remarried and bore a son.
Malinali,
herb, white feathered fan, yarn of a riber
stood next in the throne's shadow.
Tenepal, with a mother's love
sought her son, not her daughter
to ascend the throne.
Malinali,
headstrong and proud
was not her mother's daughter
but her father's heart.

Malinali
was a woman.

II

Birthright stolen
Malinali
was sold to merchants.
Indentured, she travelled everywhere

with these pochtecas.
In Tabasco, they sold her to the chief of Chocan.
She learned Mayan with the ease
of survival and her exceptional skills
earned her property and the suffix, tzing.

Malinali became Malintzin.

III

There were always men
in her life. This time, Cortez.
And she, the most gifted in the Mayan
king's seraglio, was the gift,
along with nineteen others.
Baptized the next dawn by Friar De Olemedo,

Malinali-Malintzin became Marina.

IV

Skills, linguistic too,
brought her to Cortez's attention.
She became his interpreter.

Was this the choice?
Did she become the pot mixer?
Liberator of those under the crushing

hand of the Aztecs?
Or traitor to her people, selling her soul
and the souls of those who had sold her?

V

And for Marina, what gift?
The name La Malinche. A volcano. An old house
decaying by the sea. The scorn of her people.
A son, Don Martin Cortez,
prime meztizo, the first begotten son.
And death as a woman.

*

Through her heart, His sorrow sharing
All His bitter anguish bearing,
Lo! the piercing sword had passed!

STATION III

Jesus Falls the First Time

V: We adore you, O Christ, and we bless you
R: Because by Your holy Cross, You have redeemed the world.

Consider this first fall of Jesus under His Cross.

My Beloved Jesus, it is not the weight of the Cross, but my sins which made you suffer so much pain.

Memoriam I

The picture of La Malinche
on an imagined movie poster
wears the face of Salma Hayek,
and all the lust of Sophia Loren.

This is my knife

Here, the cloth my mother wove

From yarn I spun

This movie poster Marina is all
we dare. Gorgons are too frightening
to contemplate; mutilated by our fear.

This? This is a needle of bone
threading like marrow

In truth, she was a child.
Fifteen, when given to Cortez

This is bread, soft as my body.
Here. Take it. A memory.

from a people who bought her
when she was barely five.

This? A jar of oil, seasoned
By my hand

But this is what men are like.

Here. Dip your bread. A memory.

This? This is the stone
Where I ground myself away.

Touch it. Touch me.
Knife. Cloth. Needle. Bread. Oil. Stone.

I will not die.
This is the memory of me.

*

O, how sad, and sore distressed,
Now she, that Mother Blessed
Of the sole-begotten One.

STATION IV

Jesus meets His sorrowful Mother

V: We adore You, O Christ, and we bless You.
R: Because by Your holy Cross, You have redeemed the world.

Consider the meeting of the Son and the Mother, which took place on this journey.

My most loving Jesus grant me the grace of a truly devoted love for Your most holy Mother.

Memoriam II

I

I am this stone in the middle of the road.
Blessed by the fall of her sweat,
by the fall of her sorrow,
as she walks this life's path.

I am a shadow
in the window
waiting

II

I am this seed kicked by her feet
I am this seed; I am this star.
Where does night stop being light?
Where does love cease to be anything but this?

I am the dust settling
on the artifacts of your life
Barely leaving a trace

III

Did he ever touch her face in public?
Or was that particular tenderness a place
he never travelled to? This much
I can tell: *It is hard to remain human.*

The slight depression
in the chair
watching you sleep at night

IV

I suppose you could say that.
But candles will burn with the pleasure
of their own crackling.
And if the incense censer is God's pipe,
how lazy of him not to get his own vices.

I am a ghost
made by your shame
wishing my dead were here
to save me

V

Her silence watches me; stoic
as a mud granary guarding a night field.
And no one else I've known died of love.
Still this is her inheritance: This patch of sky
shredded by swallow's wings; and my art.

I cradled your words
to my breast
Lie by lie
But all children must
be weaned

*

Woebegone, with heart's prostration
Mother meek, the bitter Passion
Saw she of her glorious Son.

STATION V

Simon Helps Jesus to carry the Cross

V: We adore you, O Christ, and we bless you
R: Because by Your holy Cross, You have redeemed the world.

Consider Simon the Cyrenian, constrained to carry the Cross behind our Lord.

My dear Jesus, I will not refuse the Cross as the Cyrenian did.

Note to Self (I)

It tastes like something.
All of it.

Remember Susan said to you after your reading –

I thought these poems were about women.

No, you said. They are about ghosts.
The evacuation of women.
No, you said, they are about men.

No, you said.

This is what they are.

These Poems.

*

Who could mark, from tears refraining,
Christ's dear Mother uncomplaining
In so great a sorrow bowed?

STATION VI

Veronica wipes the Face of Jesus

V: We adore you, O Christ, and we bless you
R: Because by Your holy Cross, You have redeemed the world.

Consider how the holy woman Veronica presented Him with a towel, with which He wiped His adorable face.

My beloved Jesus, Your face was beautiful before, but in this journey it has lost all its beauty.

The Annunciation

Candles gutter under the intensity of her gaze
dispelling a votive passion; fire,
into dripping wax; yet hot.

Perdóname mi amor, estoy débil.

This was not the annunciation she had planned.
No fallen angel to lead her by the hand
between nodded sleep and counted breath,

each precious, holding the measure
of her prayer, the unspoken. Desire,
the hush between bell-tolls, falls softer than morning.

Once chasing butterflies into a field
she came upon subjects who bowed. That moment,
she wished insignificance was all she had.

Perdóname mi amor, estoy débil.

Night settles in blue, warming itself
to the full-bodied black of good coffee
on the unsteady flames of the votive candles.

She gathers her rosary with the echo of pebbles
collected on the edge of pagan Sundays by a meditative
sea, their smoothness the real thing.

The assurance: life will become more life. Unbroken
circles or curves hold it with heartbreaking tenderness,
yet with the power to defy time; eternal.

Perdóname mi amor, estoy débil.

But there are things that can only be
approximated, like the curve of a bowl,
the dance of tomorrow, new life, new hope.

She would hold him, withholding from him
even as his wave overwhelmed her rock.
Struggling to be brave, this time, she would whisper.

Perdóname mi amor, estoy débil.

*

Who, unmoved, beheld her languish,
Underneath His cross of anguish,
'Mid the fierce, unpitying crowd?

STATION VII

Jesus falls the second Time

V: We adore You, O Christ, and we bless You.
R: Because by Your holy Cross, You have redeemed the world.

Consider the second fall of Jesus under the Cross.

My most gentle Jesus, how many times You have pardoned me!

The Dream of the Rood

I

La Llorona; in the darkness of arteries, she lurks
with the patience of a fermenting hate.
Denial is key to eradication, so her face first
is obliterated, the empty hug of her cowl's shadow,
and all we see is the sum of our terror –
Nails, long and silvery in the imagined moonlight.

I am the wood of your lives, your windhold,
your lintel, your chair, your board, your death,
your life, your bed. The post of a mid-day's yawning
lean. I am the wood of your lives. The hearth, the fire,
the smoke, the warmth, the cross, the sacrifice.

I am the wood of your lives, crossroad in complex grain.
I hold the sacrifice of your days, the dreams of your nights,

the blood of your fear, the greed of your offering,
your garden's
lost delight. Pillar of day, post of night, the wood
of your lives.
Ah, smoke me to nothingness.

II

A river of sighs pours from the cut,
everything belonging to the heart. Desire
mixing with blood in this season of milk.
The world is filled with the death of a single woman.
And nothing encompasses the moment.
Not a homeless woman shuffling behind a cart,
nor words like truth, beauty or even genocide.
The moon on wet tarmac is a lie.

III

This is the measure of my faith –
A coyote circling my car three times,
Joshua trees falling back from the road,
this land reclaiming me in rock and
I bite down on this lie and swallow.
If this death proves anything – there is power
even in the words of an ordinary woman.

*

For His people's sins rejected,
She her Jesus, unprotected,
Saw with thorns, with scourges rent.

STATION VIII

The Women of Jerusalem weep over Jesus

V: We adore You, O Christ, and we bless You
R: Because by Your holy Cross, You have redeemed the world.

Consider how those women wept with compassion at seeing Jesus in such a pitiable state.

My Jesus, laden with sorrows, I weep for the offences I have committed against You.

Alchemy of Fire

Seeing the fascination of fire
in the child's eye, she floated the candle's stub
across the fountain's wave. It rode
on the upside-down picture
of the Virgin of the Sacred Heart,
accompanied by the ripples of her song.
The storm brewing, the crossing unleashed
in a whip's lick across her back;
and then the hanging.

Suspended, she saw only the fascination
of death in the child's eye.
Fighting the rope's bite, she sung
it to the refuge of a heartbeat's shadow.

*

Saw her Son from judgment taken,
Her belov'd in death forsaken
Till His Spirit forth He sent.

STATION IX

Jesus Falls the Third Time

V: We adore You, O Christ, and we bless You.
R: Because by Your holy Cross, You have redeemed the world.

Consider the third fall of Jesus Christ.

My outraged Jesus, give me strength sufficient to conquer all human respect.

Towards Haunting

There is the contradiction of forests.   Though you have the wand
Sorrow tender with the regret of rain –   we hold the world
and salt is the taste of the fall.   our womb

What if I carve my name into temple steps,   Though you point
draw my faith in stone, on every wall?   we are the destination
Things without a name are terrifying.

Yet grass can hold the rain in fluted stems.   Though you rage like storms
If the soul exists, why does it not haunt
evil's sleep, the nightmare of its killer?   we are the power

How it dissipates in the faith of light.
Waves on the beach wash meditatively.   Though you still grow
Lengthening with evening's stretch,   we wear the face of God

licking the last of light
from the walls, return the ghosts.

*

Fount of love and holy sorrow
Mother, may my spirit borrow
Somewhat of your woe profound

STATION X

Jesus Is Stripped of His Garments

V: We adore You, O Christ, and we bless You
R: Because by Your holy Cross, You have redeemed the world.

Consider the violence with which the executioners stripped Jesus.

My innocent Jesus, help me strip myself of all affection to things of earth.

Note to Self (II)

[These are the facts]

I should know, I have read
all the books on the subject.

And if she lived in a small English village?
With a name like La Malinche?
Not hardly.
A woman with her reputation?
Frankly I don't know
what to think.

What is the measure of a heart torn?
We pause and listen to time passing.

Gather all the desiccated hearts.
Smoke them in a fire
until they become nothing –
only hot breath on night's face.

Ah, let them grieve, let them.

What can you say about a life you cannot
remember?
Yet remember this life you cannot speak,
or speak as a lie.

But this much is true:
I have only lied to those I love.

*

Unto Christ, with pure emotion,
Raise my contrite heart's devotion,
Love to read in every wound.

STATION XI

Jesus is nailed to the Cross

V: We adore You, O Christ, and we bless You
R: Because by Your holy Cross, You have redeemed the world.

Consider how Jesus offered to His Eternal Father the sacrifice of His death for our salvation.

My Jesus! loaded with contempt, nail my heart to Your feet.

The Golden Bough

We are born like this:
melancholy; the call of a lost gull
tearing night with the burn of it,

cracking our wings to the dust
of old parchments stored in caves,
falling, grain by grain.

And death can come like this.
In slow increments.
But sometimes, we feel

it necessary to preface
it with a thunderstorm, rain washing
in an imagined purity.

And this is the nub:

we oft think vision the bigger.
Everything a landscape can see.
But sound fills spaces not yet dreamed.

*

Those five wounds on Jesus smitten,
Mother! in my heart be written,
Deep as in your own they be.

STATION XII

Jesus is Raised Upon the Cross, and Dies

V: We adore You, O Christ, and we bless You
R: Because by Your holy Cross, You have redeemed the world.

Consider how Jesus, after three hours' Agony on the Cross, bows His head, and dies.

O my dying Jesus, I kiss devoutly the Cross on which You died for love of me.

Sunlight

The old woman dies on the sunny porch.
Feeble hands, palms up in lap, collect what
light she can, for the darkness to cross.

*

You, my Saviour's Cross who bear,
And your Son's rebuke who share,
Let me share them both with you!

STATION XIII

Jesus is taken down from the Cross

V: We adore You, O Christ, and we bless You
R: Because by Your holy Cross, You have redeemed the world.

Consider how Joseph and Nicodemus, took Him down from the Cross, and placed Him in the arms of His afflicted Mother.

O mother of sorrow, for the love of this Son, accept me for your servant, and pray to Him for me.

Elegy

A country churchyard, but no elegy   My blood is the cry of water
for the dead. My feet scuff their faces.   unable to slake its own thirst.
Ten thousand Chumash feed this soil, souls
marked only by the flowers they push up.   Imagine a love this complete –

Dare.
And the rest is death, and only death.   Imagine it, compressed between:
Fear?

The one who lived with birds, Juana Maria,
her true name lost to all but dolphins,   But mine is not a quiet grave.
sighs to the wind from the black plaque   It sits on the hillside of the heart
with an embossed compass, riveted to stone.
collecting something that is not dust,
And the rest is death, and only death.   halo darker than a monk's cowl.

If I could match the rage of prophets
I would call down fire; righteous, righteous fire.   And there are no names
In the softness of skin, I turn to my lover.   for the things we carry to the grave.

If only I could wear her heart next to mine.
And love is a cannibalistic feast. The oarsman must be paid.
But the rest is death, and death alone. Your heart, poeta, the levy.

*

In the Passion of my Maker,
Be my sinful soul partaker,
Weep till death, and keep with you

STATION XIV

Jesus is laid in the Sepulchre

V: We adore You, O Christ, and we bless You
R: Because by Your holy Cross, You have redeemed the world.

Consider how the disciples carried the body of Jesus to bury it, accompanied by His holy Mother.

Oh, my buried Jesus, I kiss the stone that encloses you.

In The House of Spirits

I

A house alone by the sea
A house on a bluff overlooking the sea
All around, the ghostly call of waves to unrelenting
stone, like time beating itself to death
on the indifference of the universe

A Love Frustrated

II

This house lonely by the sea
This house on a bluff overlooking the sea
has no roof, and though weathered walls sun
in this brightness, the damp fills it all –
this house, this bluff, this day, this sea

Un amor frustrado.

*

Mine with you be that sad station,
There to watch the great Salvation
Wrought upon th' atoning Tree.

BUFFALO WOMEN

"Word by word,
we beat the love
out of each other."

— Yusef Komunyakaa

I

Dearest Jane,

Even as I pen this, the train is whistling into the depot
bearing fresh fodder for this mad, mad war.
That sound, melancholy, like a lost starling,
always accompanies the gentle fall of evening.
Candles are rationed and our wicks are no more,
the last of the light is my only illumination as I write,
fast as a field hand racing against the coming dark.
Were that you were here, no doubt my very soul, not
just my tent, should be illumined by the gentle fire
of your affections. I have been compelled
by the argument and the insistence of my commanding
officer to leave my all negro platoon and follow him
to his new posting as the Captain of an all white platoon.
Imagine that, Jane, the only negro amongst all that white
and them never guessing my deeper secret.
Our orders are to proceed to the front,
though I wish they were to repair home to you,
to the more natural plodding of my past.
Sweet Jane, I feel myself much changed
by the heady scent of sweat and dried
blood that settles like a fog over our camp.
The frenzy of killing is a delirium that drives us,
relentless as my old master's cracker drove me. My
love, it was not my intent to let this vulgar life
into the more gentle innocence of yours.
Remember always that I love you.

Sincerely

Henri

II

Dear Henri,

Your letters are more precious than life to me.
They do much to assuage my fear of losing you,
though it is never fully allayed. The space between
each one is like a slow agonizing death, and I
worry for you so. Why insist on this stubbornness?
You have only to reveal your mortal wound to the medics
and they will discharge you into my loving arms.
You may still receive a pension and, no matter if not,
we have always managed with the farm.
I cannot imagine the terrifying spectacles
that you are witness to, although in your sweetness
you do try to share them, your words betray the difficulty.
Promise me that you will strive always to be safe.
Remember the bird of paradise you planted?
Well it has spread in the garden, so that it looks like
a gaggle of tropical birds have gone berserk.
It would amuse you nearly as much as the time the jacaranda
trees coated the front yard in a carpet of lavender petals,
and you rolling in them for hours.
I am enclosing some rags to staunch your blood
and a long piece of sheet to swaddle yourself.

Hurry home my love.

Jane

III

Dearest Jane,

Flesh is a curious thing. To the eye
it does appear seamless and in that thinking stronger
than any metal. Yet this wondrous creation, once
the seam is ripped, lets out all the fluid of its living
absorbing instead death. The way a fish on land fears
the emptying of water, draws in air. The impulse to be filled,
to be full of something, anything, seems to drive this odd
beast. Yesterday I killed my first man.
Rammed my bayonet into him with such ferocity,
that I drove him back five feet. Dropping his rifle,
his mouth opened in surprise as death filled him.
And I loved it. The trembling that began in my stomach,
rushed up to the back of my head, then down to the rise of
my pubis. Causing the hair to rise deliciously. It felt
wholesome, profound. The epiphany, like the taste of
blood on the tongue. Or earth. Dank. Damp.
Later, behind some bushes, as I hunched to change rags
and burn the old one, I wiped the still bleeding blade
of my bayonet, feeling the trembling return,
stronger this time, as my blood mingled
with that of the soldiers who had died at its point.
This feeling Jane, was something new, something feral,
like the single purpose of a single moment.

Yours truly,

Henri

IV

Sweetest Henri,

I know we promised to be honest,
one to the other, but your recent missive,
though welcome as any epistle from you,
filled me with a dread that clung
like dampness to wet wood. I am terrified
for your immortal soul, dear sweet Henri.
This mad war of Lincoln is infecting you
with a sickness too depraved to even address.
I have gathered in some herbs,
remembered from childhood with my Aunt Tilly.
I will use them to spice the candles I light
every night with my prayers. I must be careful
because, whilst they are wholesome with my love,
there are those who will tar it witchcraft.
God knows we need no more stigmas attached to us,
or for the town to examine us more closely.
Yesterday, Rev. Pickering spoke highly of your manhood;
it was all I could do to keep from laughing.
The Wilson farm was raided,
marauders slaughtering every living creature.
They were a sight, scattered there like the senseless
pieces of a broken vase. To avert the same fate,
I sold our creatures, buying gold dust in their stead,
which I hid in the stem of your pipe.
It lies there, forlorn, a wretch awaiting its master.
Some evenings I sit before the fire, puffing
on its unlit stem, my lips to yours.

Always your heart,

Jane

V

Dearest Sweet Jane,

I woke with the taste of your apple pie in my mouth,
carried over no doubt from my dreams.
It made me realize how much I miss you and our home.
Though I think that dreams are really the place
for such memories, as my old life seems
to be no more than a dream. Being
up earlier than everyone else, a gift made
possible by the dream of you, I was able to wash
in the river naked. Removing all my garments and bindings,
I felt my body sigh like a flower opening to the sun.
The relief of it was immeasurable.
I sank gratefully into the embrace of the water,
the break between the surface and depth of it
producing tiny waves, like a mouth kissing my nipples.
Teasing the way you always do, first with your hair
then your lips, remember? I confess that my hand
found my tenderness and the release
was like the sun on water.
I have been thinking my love, and on my return,
I would like to reveal the truth of us, of myself.
I am tired of this restrictive masculine role.
Write soon, my love.

Yours truly,

Henri

VI

My sweet Henri,

I do feel very guilty. So much
time has elapsed between your last letter.
It is the fault of a wicked illness making the rounds,
once infected it seems impossible to shake
the clammy hand of death it brings.
Mrs. Wilcox has passed from it, as has the young
Harding boy. I thought it best to stay put and not
venture into town. Making a reply impossible to post.
I find myself going to church more these days,
to beseech that you be kept safe. I know
you will scoff at this, but it brings me much comfort
so I will continue to do it. Repeat Psalm 23 daily.
My Aunt Tilly used to take a decoction of dried
St. John's Wort, a curious but amazing root.
I am enclosing some here. It really raises the spirit
and I have much hope it will help you by and by.
I know hope is indeed too unformed a thing to ask
you to hold onto, but at times like these, it the best
we can ask for ourselves. I have enough hope
for us both, my love. I flushed when I read
your last letter and confess I return to it on retiring
most nights. I miss you terribly, my heart, and keep a lamp
lit every night in the window to guide you home,
safe and with a heart of love.

Your wife,

Jane.

VII

Dear Jane,

I read somewhere that the world we see is new
only once, in the innocence of infancy.
The rest is just the recall of memory.
Were that it were true, I would not feel like
the wretch I know I am become.
This infernal conflict is no place for a soul
as delicate as mine, and I say that while
still claiming the equal of any man.
Now, more than before, I realize that we cannot
but be changed by it, learning new things daily.
Constantly the natural world around us, and
the impure stain of our own nature,
acts upon us so as to make us this way.
I killed more men today. Not with the distance
of a musket shot or the justice of a sword.
This was something entirely different.
I clubbed them to death with my rifle stock.
Beat them with the confidence of a Chinese
laundry woman. Until their bodies yielded
red to my cleansing. All the time,
I grunted, moaned even. The sound low
and sweet at the back of my throat. Clubbing
until each one was still, then panting.
I gulped for air, sweating, alive, so alive.
Then laughing like a coyote circling something
dying slowly in the desert, I took a deep breath
and moved forward. The killing never stops.
I am afraid of what I am becoming, Jane.

Henri

VIII

Dear Jane,

It has been a while since your last letter
and I am worried about you. Where are you?
I am kept awake by my fear that
something unspeakable has befallen you.
I am keeping as well as I can, given the circumstances
here. We are trapped, pinned down on one side
by the weather – snow and a frozen river
that may not bear the full burden –
and on the other by the hatred of the enemy,
which is preferable to the indifference of snow.
We have taken some heavy cannons and
the horizon is filled with splintered trees grinning
like teeth in a skull. To give you a true sense
of the troubling scenes I have witnessed is beyond
my power and I scarce think you would believe me.
Suffice it to say that the devil returns
among us nightly, dancing between the tents
of freezing hungry men. In the lazy sunlight of day,
there is much talk too evil to recount here,
taking shape in covetous stares aimed at the old, weak
and dying. There is something malevolent brewing
in our very souls. A thing so heinous
that should we wish to return from it, we could not
devise a path home. With a growing dread,
I realize that I am not immune from it.
Pray for my immortal soul, sweet Jane. Pray!

Yours truly,

Henri

IX

Dearest Jane,

I have not heard from you in a long time,
nor you from me. I realize
that we are sealed off by weather and the war
as surely as though we were butterflies
wrapped in the silk of those cocoons you love
so, calling them beautiful, holy.
We are all dizzy from hunger here, and emaciated.
So wasted have I become that I no longer need
my chest binding. I am truly one of the men.
You would not recognize me, my love.
My face is harrowing even to crows.
The older and dying soldiers have been tagged
crones by the rest of us. We watch them
with guarded eyes and they can feel it coming:
this hunger that must take shape soon.
They huddle together like ancient birds,
eyes darting, calculating every movement we make.
And daily our circle about them grows tighter,
pulled by the spasms of hunger-taut bellies.
So far, it is only the shame of daylight, and night
fires that keep it in. But how long before
this desperate wickedness overruns the qualms
of good people? Before the desire for the smell
of cooking meat, the softness of flesh, breaks us all?
This is an unspeakable horror, Jane,
and I would surely be hanged for telling you.
You will never read this and for that, I am grateful.

Yours truly,

Henri

X

Dear Jane,

I suspect this letter will never feel
the gentle grace of your hands,
nor will you read these words.
The snow shows no signs of letting up,
and the cold is worse even than the night terrors,
its icy hold claiming fingers and limbs as though
devouring us one appendage at a time.
My wound has dried up, the flow no doubt frozen
by this infernal weather or perhaps even the hunger.
We have begun to boil our spare boots along with salt
and the few spices Cook has left.
The leather is too tough to eat, but the soup
has enough of the taste of meat to fool our hunger
momentarily. We bulk up on tree bark.
Today we made a charge at the enemy.
It was halfhearted and we failed
to do more than drive them a few yards back.
But they too are so debilitated
they could not mount a successful counter.
Neither side it seems can muster the mettle to succeed.
We always return to the problem of finding food.
All the horses and mules are long gone,
the marrow picked clean from the bones.
I swear one can play them like a flute.
Even the crows have deserted us in fear.
Today our captain gave a rousing speech about how
it was our duty to stay alive and enjoined us not to falter
in that duty. The abyss is calling, sweet Jane.

Henri

XI

Dearest Jane,

And this is how it is done.
We chased down the oldest crone last night.
It was no sport, and despite their sprightliness
born of terror, the hunt took only a few moments.
The other crones all pulled tight into balls,
dark stones in the purity of snow. Even in the dark,
we could see the widening of the crone's eyes,
the recognition that pleading was futile.
Four men held it down, ripping its clothes off.
It was no more than a bag of bones, but to us it was plump
as a new calf. Its squirming and pig-like
squeals enjoined no pity from us, but a desperate anger.
We circled in clumps of twos and threes, hugging
the shadows as far from the fire as possible,
our shame compounded by hunger and anger;
and then mercifully the sergeant ran his sword through
the crone, slicing from chest to navel,
viscera steaming in the snow.
The chaplain and captain turned away in disgust.
But what could they do? The confusion
that followed was suddenly comical;
nobody knew how to cook it.
Our curse is our endless resourcefulness for evil
and the night was soon heavy
with the deliciousness of cooking meat,
and while the crone dripped fat into the fire,
we mimicked the noises it made before dying.
And so we have become.

Henri

XII

Dearest Jane,

I received my first letter from you
in nearly three months. I cannot measure my joy
at your tender words. Along with your letter,
spring has thawed winter's internment
and we have moved even further forward.
Our resourcefulness allowed us to find food
during the winter months while the enemy starved
for the lack of it. We were able to launch attack
after attack on them. We left the dead where they fell
and now in spring's thaw; they have emerged from the snow
like the wanton pieces of the broken jar your missive speaks of.
There were causalities on our side too,
but nothing near the losses suffered by the South.
The chaplain and captain recommended our battalion
be disbanded and the soldiers sent to new postings.
This last winter was harsh on our conscience
and everyone feels it best to forget.
I wrote you several letters in that long darkness,
none of which survived to be sent to you.
I laughed when I read of you puffing on my unlit pipe
stuffed with gold-dust. What a remarkable creature you are.
I have decided that I want no more of this war,
and revealed myself to the doctor whose lust
weighed my breasts before discharging me.
I will be home soon. You are my redemption, sweet Jane.

Yours truly,

Henrietta.

from

THERE ARE NO NAMES FOR RED

Like a piece of ice on a hot stove, the poem must ride
on its own melting

— Robert Frost

I

The way desire is a body eroding
into a pile of salt marked by a crown of birds –
and black. This fall is not rain, grain too subtle
for that dissolution. A constellation wrapped
in a stitch spreading like sand charting
thread across time a tender weave
and hope. This is resurrection.

II

And the sky is red
                    And the moon
And light is this rain.

This is all the terror we can bear:

          the moment between flame
and where shadow begins
          but only so much as can be cupped
in a child's palm

and yet to say: the loved one
          has slipped to ghost.

III

What attempts survival here has no words
but hunger. A white backcloth that devours
the blackening. Then red cut in lines thick
as paste and obscuring the once figurative.
This desire wears cerements of yellow and sun.
And at the edge of this world, a box of wood
and canvas: light and light and light.

IV

Everything here can so easily turn to mud
and the recalcitrance of dead leaves and bugs.
There is hair here too. Not so much brown and animal
as rough; I speak now of sorrow, of weight
beyond measure. There is a drowned woman
in the dark swirl. This paint, buoyant and light, eddies.

V

Whatever guilt drives this brush is nocturnal and heavy
with the smell of the cramped darkness under the stairs.
But night will not be blamed. What good are words
when the green light over the ocean is all we need?

VI

What passes for night here has more to do with the place
where the body is flayed open to sorrow and wonder.
The boy on the bridge drops a feather into a lost river.
A rusting lawn dreams of grass rude and fescue.
A match held down to tobacco still burns with an upward flame.
There is no truth here.
Dutifully the mist comes down the mountain. What else can I tell you?

VII

That lone shoe on the curb, foot turned to the wind, the road south.
Snow complicates the purity. Snow, what do we know of this?
Sand, sand and grains that rub. Persistence and the silt.
That eternal shifting that erases all that it builds.

VIII

Winter is defeated by a flock of geese flying towards the sun.
The sea is only as lonely as a single conch, or a sand dollar
fritted away on an impossible dream. Even this bold black line.
The Igbo believe the sun is only the aura of a creature we have
no name for. What is song here is ritual in another language.

IX

My first death was a butterfly.
The smell of Earl Grey mocks Proust.
But you're 39 now, she said. Do you still need
that hurt little boy? This line flowers up like a tree
in a red night but curves with the weight of lynching.
How can the moon be so blind?
Blake on Paxil? No tygers burning, that's for sure.
Noncommittal lines that won't speak to each other and yet
the narrow gutter between them overflows
with the dirty water of all that is unsaid.
Will my marriage last this long too?
In rooms without names, Aga Shahid
Ali is still mourned with a circling grief.

X

When I returned from Auschwitz brimming with sorrow
and love, I said I will write a poem so profound it will
core the earth like an apple. Instead all I can say is:
daisies have grown over the train tracks and a sparrow
lays blue eggs high in a tree like an incinerator chimney.
But I could be lying. We all do it.
Percival's cat was called Cat.
Look closely at that painting. See the outline of her x-rays?
Jim was the Crow he carried on his left shoulder.
It grew strong and flew away but left a heavier weight.

XI

That woman in a New York café cannot escape what it means
to sound like a Boer. If I were a better man, I would have compassion.
The thing is this: the dead won't stay buried. Emily said, about the woman
on the bus, she said are you going to the other side?
How easy it is for light reflecting off a polished wood floor to bend
    into metaphor.
Fire, water and mud. What a curious way to make a body.
Gravity wasn't the apple to Newton's head and yet he claims discovery.
But the moment you point to the black dog shivering against the red door
in the relentless rain, you lose it.

XII

Goldsworthy arranges daisies, a meditation in the crook of the stream
with all the awe of the Neanderthal burying their dead.
The water takes the gift.
Is this how you get fish to make butter?
I remember every detail of everything my father inflicted on me
to erase his fear of loving me. I walk
the stations of that pain with all the relish of a self-flagellating
monk. I know something of pilgrimage.

XIII

Crocodiles in the river remind us every gift is hard won.
Perhaps it is the mud that makes the arrow-tips of rice so green.
The problem with caves is that we must enter them.
Ghosts in the morning rain. When it is over,
the rain is never enough.
Of course I hated the Mau Mau growing up. They killed
women who looked like my mother.
They wore the face of my father. I have to
throw this baby out with the bathwater.

XIV

In the end it just happens.
Reasons are only logs to bank the fire of hope.
In Rwanda, before the genocide, the word for rape was the same
    as marriage.
The idea of gestural fragments.
These are the spells, these are the spells.
The ghosts of washing drying on the line, like birds weaned at home.
The urge is to migrate, restless.
Some of our truest conversations are in diners.
My hands have known this experience –
the making and breaking of my spirit in this craft.
Held.
In the nebulous frame of words.
Those stormy symphonies of Beethoven.
Figures of impossible dimensions.

XV

There is something soft here. Smooth as a stone in water.
A trick of the light perhaps, or this; the cold nonchalance
of fate and all the beauty is nothing more than this
canvas this skin and the hope we covet.

XVI

Also in other non-intended ways but touching. Canvas
heavy with salt after salt and salt and water,
the brine a knowledge and this sail unannealed like skin
and my grandmother dying, dying in the shower and water
all around her. This is not intended and yet the distance between
almost perfect and complete chaos is a hair's breath.
Loose strands unravel and follow an idea.
In Berlin there are brass caps, square and green with time,
set into the paving stones that trip you.
You look down and see the names of those taken to the camps.
Stubbing stones they call them. *Stolpersteine*. And nobody knows
exactly who put them there. Turkish women in black
descend on us like a gaggle of crows. Yes, I said gaggle.
And what is gained? And what is lost?
What begs silence here is beyond even that.

XVII

There is no doubt, kin is my search. I want to connect these lines
to the ones charting my face in the faded mirror of time. This need
is visceral.
And yet ideas are robust as plump well-fed geese and this is the lie of it.
I don't seek kin here. I seek adoration. I seek worship. I seek the voice
of my father.
First of all, I do not buy into mythological figures, so fuck Odin
and his tree.
Wounded trees mark the spot, an itch unreachable. But still gazing,
Odin summons
the runes. I say futhark, you say tomatoes. And the deep is this dark mark
across the soul.
This poem is an animal, Terence says and sips some coffee. That way
language can
sprint across the desert filling it with an oasis. And why not?
This pure flame, this pure fire, and these scars our nomadic natures
carve across us.
If this poem is an animal it's all Percival's fault. If this poem is
an animal.

XVIII

Under a relentless sun in a small Mexican town, three old women
in black gather before the startled white of the church.
A little girl watches from across the street.
If a newspaper falls from the hand of an old man dying
in a chair, fanning into a tarot spread on the floor and
no one is there to see it, does it make a sound?

XIX

My grandfather once said the Milky Way is God's clock.

XX

A taxi through night and palms that gather desire like dew.
A window opens onto the hiss of rain on tarmac and this smell
is old earth, and a grave, grace even and flowers rotting
at the edge of time, at the edge of the road where a child died.
It's like the way the little white plane hovers on the vastness of
the ocean between Godthab and St. John's. The Atlantic tamed
momentarily by the flight information screen and yet in the dark cabin,
all that keeps it aloft is the soft breathing of the other sleeping passengers.
And nothing is lonelier in the world at this moment
than that little white cross on the expanse of blue screen.
Faith is something like this, I imagine. Not of God. But of a pen or a brush
held up like the last flaming torch of the century, and yet flimsy –
this desire of the artist to keep the blue from swallowing it all up.
Like something that happens only at night.
Like a lie and desperation so thick you can breath it. Moments
like this, the skin widens to the lover's touch and the back arches
to whispers.
Even this cannot keep the void away. The mid-Atlantic ridge is a
mountain under the sea, and its active volcanoes widen the ocean bed.
I want to say, "This one's on me, Mr. Freud! Can I get an Amen?"
Still we're lost in that vast blue and I think how did the Vikings ever find
anything down there? Stumbling about in the dark like still unrealized id's.
There is nothing clear about it, nothing lasting about this clarity.
I will do it different, I say. I will. As if the threat of death is not a smell
I will lose in a few days. This terror comes in without knocking.
Like a familiar lover intruding into the bathroom as I pee.
I will lose even this when it mingles with the old smell of her wetness
and I will forget and drown us both in wine and regret.

XXI

This thing is a too exclusive love for colour,
a burden on the canvas. Something Jesus would get
but only as Muddy Waters screaming in a riot of shadows.

XXII

There is a blur of black on green like the unruly shadow of some night be-
fallen building, a shawl wrapped around a hooker's too tight
too short skirt.
Or the contrite line of an old nun bent black from shame and
the pleasure of beads rubbed between sensuous fingers and the prayers
savoured like divine sweatmeats. Or perhaps it is just me, or the dark
glimpse I catch from the corner of my fearful eye. Or death.
Ah, but the green fescue grass and the dark of loam.

XXIII

To be sure there are lines, shapes and swirls of colour even.
Like Van Gogh it is what is not alive that lives here.
Imaginary trees in the throes of convulsions and a compulsion
that is totemic not atavistic. Though
there is sacrifice, there is compassion too.
And this is why we fear spiders. In a pinch they will outsmart us.
See this knife. This knife is dull. This knife pulls a jagged wish
through oils as thick as butter. This knife is sacrifice.
This knife is the priest.
Percival's heart bleeds on a stiff white canvas window.

XXIV

There is a green one above my desk.
Ripe, viridity fairer than lime and yet darker.
Across this plain, this light-undulating moor, a scream.
Like a bird of paradise gone wild. Some nights,
when I look up suddenly, I am back in a cell and my fear
chokes me and then my guilt. Indulging tears
I feel rather than see
this young boy, this ghost,
clear his throat in disgust and leave the room.
What is hard here is beyond the romance of words.

XXV

In Mexico City's metro, my friend tells me, is a stop called Ethiopia.
Just that. And a lion's profile stamped into the concrete walls.
There are catacombs honeycombing the world.

XXVI

Someone please tell Carlos Drummond de Andrade that there
    is a stone
in the middle of the road. I saw it too, finally.
Carlos has been looking for that stone since my grandmother
borrowed it to sharpen her knife. It was the onions, you see.
My knife wasn't so sharp either the day I cut the throat on my childhood.
It's not hard to kill a childhood.
Did you never see your father slap your mother?
Did you never feel the shame?
Never thought, yes, shut up, Mum?
Did her eyes never forgive you?
Cats are easier to forgive. Even when their rabid bite
costs you twenty-six injections to the stomach.
Riding her bike in the slight drizzle each knee catching in my throat
the young woman and white. The flash of underwear and I am six again.

XXVII

How nicely they've fixed the bullet holes in the walls,
in Rwanda. Painted bright petals around some areolas.

XXVIII

A painting is never the thing it says it is.
Of course this is poetry, every human breath is sublime.
Ask Paolo. In cold caves, with the instance of a flash he captures
only a breath. And then another. Clouds of blue and hope.
This is a sculpture, he says. Even this. I believe him. Percival doesn't
paint the sea. Yet all of his canvases are full of water. Maybe
I shouldn't have gotten back on the bicycle after that bad fall that crushed
my balls. You're ten, Mark said. If you don't you never will. Just do it.
Was that a Nike ad even then?

XXIX

Percival says it's not for the fishing. It's for the river. The sudden bend
that holds all the light in a man's soul. There is something like awe
in his eyes.
He looks down and takes a bite of salmon. The fish is good. Pete's is open late.
We both like that. Nocturnes.

Sometimes a goat lifts a bottle. But we always stop short of the lips.
Alcohol goes better with Pisces. We have none of their grace.

XXX

In the end, there are no names for red but fire,
hydrant, apple, ball, heart, blood, sacrifice, and altar.
Look, my nephew says, fire engine.

from
SANCTIFICUM

Every poet is a monster
– Tomaz Salamun

…terror is a state of complete understanding…
– Larry Levis

OM

1

The hills of my childhood are purple with dusk and wings –
guinea fowl launched like a prayer to the still forming moon.
I hold Bean's shell to my ear. There is no sea. But only sea.
By my bed, in an empty chair, my shirt unwinds.
I remember my aunt counting the dead in the newspaper.
I never told anyone that every sliver of orange I ate
was preceded by words from high mass.
Per omnia saecula saeculorum.
Spit out pit. Amen.
Juice. Amen. Flesh.

2.

A full moon leaning on a skyscraper. The taste:
qat and sweets on a tropical afternoon.
The dog's black tongue was more terrifying than its teeth.
The gravestone rising out of the puddle was more sinister
than the body we discovered as children swinging
in the summer-hot orchard.

3.

The old woman singing a dirge has a voice of dust.
Sorrow lodged like a splintered bullet next to the heart.
A man once asked me in the street:
Do you own your own bones?
She likes the home I come in, I say to Cristina
as we drive towards the Golden Gate.
Bean, I repeat.
She loves the home I come in
and I am alive with fire and scars.
Here is my body, I say, eat it, do this,
Remember me –

4.

Even now melancholy is a skin flayed
and worn in dance through the city.
Yes, the city becomes skin too and wears me
as skin and I want to say; this is my body, as I stroke
the curve of the fountain in the park.
This is my blood. Drink it. Remember.
The safety of doorways is an illusion.
They lead nowhere.
This is why we build houses.
Sand, when there is no water, can ablute,
washing grain by grain even the hardest stone of sin.
But you, but you, you are a sin that I live for.
Ne Me Quitte Pas. Ne Me Quitte Pas. Ne Me Quitte Pas.
Nina Simone's voice walks in dragging bodies,
dead black men that bled unseen in the dark
of Southern nights, shaded by leaves
and the veiled eyes of hate.
And in a poem, Lucille stands in the shadow of a tree
and pours libations for our souls,
for our salt, for our gospel.

5.

Somewhere a man speaks
in the dark, voice lost to rain.
I know this hunger, this need
to make patterns, to build meaning
from detritus; also the light
and the wood floor bare but for the lone slipper
tossed carelessly to one side. I admit the lies I've told.
Look, nothing has been true
since that picture of hell on the living room wall lost its terror.
I say I want a strong woman, but unlike Neto
I cannot have the woman and the fish.
The war followed.
Children are losing their souls to the heat.
That is to say, poor American soldiers.
The rich have found a way to charge theirs to Amex.
Ask this: what is the relationship of desire to memory?
Here is a boy in the airport café, hair cropped from service.
And he closes his eyes to take a sip of coffee.
And smiles as the dark washes the desert away.

6.

Los Angeles:
A red sky and angels thick like palm trees,
and garbage blown in the wind like cars
and the gluttony of SUVs
in an endless river of traffic.
Through the dark, we say, through the dark:
but do we ever really know?
There is a man in a field and he is searching for God.
Father, he says, father.
In the distance: birds, traffic and children.
There is a blue sky. There is a sky blue with night.

The call of the earth is a primitive song,
stomping feet and broken men.
There is a blue sky. And night.
The city is a flock of lights.
The darkness of tunnels like caves is knowledge,
also mortal. Maps are like God.
They are the city yet not the city.
They contain the city but yet do not.
We trace the lines in loss.
Sometimes we find treasure.
Sometimes something fills the mind,
something at which we pause, stopped.
The way a photograph cannot remember the living.

7.

To die is to return.
To fly is to be a bird's heart.
Neither is freedom.
If it were we would have no name for it.
No language. Not even the temptation of wind
blowing a dark woman's hair away from a cliff's edge.
Instead, feathers are brought to my door everyday by mystery.
Kindling for a fire, a beacon, an epiphany I cannot light.
This is the body of Christ.
Santificum.

SACRAMENT

1.

Have you heard of the oracle of the Igbo?
The one called Chukwu? Just one word: God.
The oracle of God.
The voice of God.
The final arbitration.
Kpom kwem.
Deep in a grove of trees, the sacred lake,
and rising in the gloom and heat,
mist, the very breath of divinity.
The unbearable trepidation,
the worship, the sheer terror and earnestness
trembling the supplicants. And the priests
sitting on rocks and in trees on haunches,
silent like vultures or Rilke's unspeakable angels.
And then a pilgrim wades cautiously into the lake.
On the shore, the line of unannointed
shivers in a shared awe.
And if the petitioner is beautiful or strong,
the priests hold her under, then shackle
for slavers. In the lake, red dye bubbles up
as God smacks his lips.
And that endless line of believers near faint
with the fearsome beauty of the thought:
Please eat me too, God.
Eat me and find me worthy.
But don't let me die.

2.

There is risk in this –
Not the words, but the dreaded embodiment of light,
a sacred song. A river darker

than caverns immeasurable,
a sacred river; not all Ganga, not all Alph,
but still fire, still fire.
Before this flight, before this persistence
the soul is bare.
Holy the water.
Holy the smoke.
Holy the flame.
Holy, holy, holy.

3.

Death is a flock of blackbirds low over muddy streets
in war-torn Sarajevo. Dirt-stained walls yearn
for all that is night. Elegies fall like raw silk.
If there is a way it is here.
Salt and ash.
This is how the Igbo clean their teeth.
Grandmother grinding charcoal
coughing as the silt rises.
Then salt rubbed into the black
as though morning were trying to temper night.
Then water and a fingertip collecting the grey,
the unidentifiable finger dipping into
a mouth held open like a wound –
A thick sludge complicates my joy.
It is made of the dissolved bones and flesh
of men we buried in swamps
behind the wall of internment. Buried
in shallow graves like a hand cupped in peat,
then bodies and lime: the hiss and sizzle, and the suck
of earth filling with water.
Of swamp digesting histories and love.
Instead of a preface, instead of a requiem,
the symphony of rain fills the night
with the distracted hurry of wild horses

crossing a plateau under a threatening sky.
I am not afraid of love, or its consequence of light,
Joy intones; chant like skin, like sand, like water.

4.

There is fog this morning. On my continent
children die. African children die every day.
It's what they do.
I can still hear my mother's sewing machine
stitching the afternoon with promise. Under a tree,
in the scent of rotting fruit, I washed
bitter-leaf for dinner. Washed and squeezed.
The bitter foaming away.
Like frothy green blood from the neck of sacrifice.
A dog is barking at spirits in the heat.
Language escapes me still – see it sprinting
down the street. Crazed. A crazy man.
Babbling. Babel. This is my language.
On a wall in Sarajevo, graffiti reads:
KILLING IS MY BUSINESS
BUSINESS IS GOOD. THE FROGMAN.
Sem gave me the book with the graffiti.
In DC, he said, my name is Sem,
eyes narrowed, even as his lips smiled.
I know this trim. A name for invisibility.
A loss for a chance to be here.
Do I not carry a pocketful of accents?
In halting speech I said it wrong: Semezdin Mehmedinovic.
He smiled as though I were singing an aria.
We went back to coffee, the dark, and rain:
a Washington DC street and the glow of lights.
Agi Mishol said, choose your rabbi carefully.
Someone who sees who you can become.
I doubt there is anything like truth here in this teashop
but the chai is good and the light on Bean is golden.

DIVINATION

1.

How can a people who have paid such a price
for life, return from the grave with such vengeance.
And who will count the Palestinian dead?
And who mourns for them? Stones and steel
and mortar bombs *will* break my bones.
In Bean's voice, Aygi returns as a girl
slender with olive in her eyes and a smile –
and snow, again snow, the cadence soft, falling.
Text message to Bean sent from my Blackberry,
Ronald Reagan Airport,
Departure Gate –
I hope you get this.
Through night and rain and a plane
things wear the musk of elegy.
And maybe even a ghost. A double
rising like light from a wet road.
By an African roadside, a woman,
more skeleton than flesh, squats.
Death wears down her resistance.
The sun tries to be merciful.

2.

I don't know why I sing
in languages I cannot understand.
Fast moving trains draw time ahead and
then there is the sea and the blue kite of horizon;
a perfect chalice for night
and the communion sliver of moon.
I am driving to Santa Barbara.
The sun this afternoon is a fallen angel, but beautiful.

Zora said, “Black people are art.”
Hallowed be thy name.
Which is to say, there is no end to ocean,
no article to limit. As for dream, he is a man
with dark robes and a gaunt face and sigh so weary
it makes the nightmare tedious. Every night he is waiting.
He doesn’t think it funny when I laugh at the crow on his shoulder.
You said mother would no longer make you sad. I believed you.
Yet over and over I wash the two dresses a woman left
after she was done with me. The smell is summer.

3.

Even in the agony of waiting –
this is the way she loves the dream.
And what woke me was the scent. Like the smell
of coffee my mother beat from the folds of her day dress.
There is a small girl shivering in a stream
as her brothers keep watch from the lip of a wooden bridge,
while behind them, mere inches from their buttocks,
cars pass. Each counted in an arc of spit, each
boy puckering fast to win the count.
Their legs kicking casually over the abyss belie their fear.
If you know sorrow, you know it hurts in the body.
I project all of my hope into the streets of South Africa.

4.

No I am not afraid of the eye chart:
in THE dmv
But i sHakE
at The Uniformed
COP who WaLks In.
My fear of uniforms is an old habit, comfortable.
Sometimes even the chief fryer at the McDonald’s can

make me break into a hot sweat if I am not expecting his glance.
Monsters don't crowd your psyche
but rather sit awkwardly on the remote control,
too polite to get up and move it, until
the constantly changing channel is unbearable.
The odds are that my political views won't stop the invasion
but to drink Ethiopian coffee during a bomb-
storm is still rebellious.

DESCENT

1.

All those demonstrations, mother,
of the Billings Ovulation Method,
aged seven, translating to women:
When your vulva swells,
before your period comes, insert –
and they, never meeting my eyes yet asking –
and for the virgins, the piece of a balloon stretched
over the lip of a coca-cola bottle was the hymen.
My mother's pen pushing against it
demonstrating pressure, pushing agonizingly,
slowly, until the virgin and I both
let our breath out in a long shuddered relief –
like a train breaking for a tunnel,
like the sun after a thunderstorm.
Who can say how much is remembered and how much invented?
Who can say what is right and wrong?
Countless good my mother did for those women
who didn't even know they could own
their own wombs or vaginas.
Even now, because I am a man,
this freedom is still academic.
Hail Mary full of grace –

Women in my childhood blackened their teeth with snuff –
it was said that men were drawn to that as much
as to the eloquence of their ample backsides –
women so strong men never got
to choose anything for them.
When did women begin to think a gentle spray
of flowers worthy of their love?
The women of my village felt their love better sated
with smoked antelope legs and baskets of bananas or yams –

children it turns out cannot eat flowers.
Yet their bodies were adorned with so much beauty.
I know they knew more than they would ever reveal to me.

2.

I have seen many red nights and purple
evenings taut with cold and winterlight,
and afternoons yellow with ripe leaves,
but I have never seen the northern lights
or a comet shower or an alien or a desert crossing
from Mexico, people loping like coyotes
in the floodlight-silver night.
Although there was an evening when rounding a bend
on a river walk in London I saw a heron lift off
and slice the silence with its snakelike head,
all wings and feathers and lapping water.
A crepuscular light, brittle like a saltine, and oh, the salt.

3.

Also it makes me pause to think that anyone could have
read Rilke and then engaged in the Holocaust.
When Ilya Kaminsky reads, the poem is wounded.
An animal crying in the face of an approaching angel
whose voice blends with its own.
Is this why Israel forgets the holocaust its people suffered
and then brings one against the Palestinians?
For Iman it is a difficult question – if we ask Israel
(and she says the name like a song, like a prayer: Is-ra-ayle)
to stop bombing the Arab, we must also condemn

the suicide bomber. For her, there is no hope for peace as long as men measure armistice in pints of blood shed on both sides, seeking an impossible balance.

PROCESSIONAL

1.

Quench the light –
and my cousin's voice heavy
with an Igbo inflection that made it a threat,
like, "I will quench you."
Like, the man quench yesterday.
Like a fragile neck breaking.
The way our ethnicity was nearly quenched in a war
that began with a pogrom against us.
Quenched and all but gone but we raged.
Still –
Igbos littered northern streets like so many dead flowers.
I trimmed the wick. The lantern gulped hungrily for life
stuttered once, twice, then gone.
Quenched.

And night, free at last, stirred, stretching, feral.
But I am still here so my blanket protected me,
the heat rash a reasonable price for safety.
The thing is, every day I was painted in calamine lotion
until I looked like a ghost, scaring myself as I went to bed.
And the world turns –
Once again rain, but not all water.
From the car window, winding up a snowy mountain pass
in Colorado, the frozen river looks like corroded copper,
all green and mottled white and the breath of time.
What a remarkable thing a voice is –
In Haiti the poor gather to protest in the slum Cite Soleil,
but no one is smiling at the irony.
I saw this old man once at the doctor's office;
he looked confused as though it was a mystery
why he had clung to life so savagely, so earnestly.

2.

A foot poised over a pool.
The surface breaks, a boy falls in,
his laughter fills the afternoon.
Ritual is the only language we truly believe in:
tea steaming a glass mug on a table,
smoke from a cigarette filling the room with blue,
the way the sun falls across our face as we sleep.
These are our things, we say.
But somewhere a door closes and another day begins.
What if the woman we have always loved,
the one we desire to wake to, is our mother?
The holy homeless fill the city like so many weeds.
Only God's children can see them.
A blue cross on a wall is a flame.
A ball falling from the sky is a meteor.
Rust is its own kind of truth:
like blood, like cities, like sunlight on a dusty road.
We never find it of course, but it's always there,
between the smoke and the flame.

3.

This is a circle song. Like songs of old.
We go over the same territory, like a mower
religiously eating grass that will grow again.
Some call it history.
The wise say it is a pond, or river.
There are things you can only say
with a canyon. Or smoke
moving across a valley towards the mist
at the foothills. I want to return
to that boy I was, but what will I say?
What would I have him do differently?
Believe in the faith of moths?

Believe in the inevitability of shadows?
This poem is like someone waiting for a bus
so long they have lost the urge to travel.
My brothers must be as tired of this as I,
dragging love as a tally board behind us,
marking off an endless but complex math
of ego and one-upmanship and debt.
But the men who came before us didn't
teach us another way.
And even when one of us summons
the courage to break the heavy wood of it
and stoke a fire of liberation,
the others chalk up more and more.
In the end, does it really matter
who started the war?
Palestine? Israel?
Iran? Iraq?
Russia? Chechnya?
The US and the rest of the world?
Break the board of death.
We are tired of tallying the wounds.

4.

Beati quorum via integra est.
Cape Town, South Africa:
Rocks sunning like whales calling to cliffs
as indifferent as teeth in an octogenarians mouth.
Dressforms in an abandoned shop haunt the night.
Note to self – look up:
Vivant.
Revenant.
Lacunae.

5.

Why would a boy who knows nothing about alchemy
and the machinations of blood and other terrors respond
to a voice calling for a rain of death and other terrors.
Red Riding Hood walks out of the forest and her basket explodes.
Count the dead spilling out of the café like rank meat thrown
to dogs in the street. Revenge begets nothing but itself.
Sometimes after a suicide bombing, flesh and bone from the dead
bomber embed themselves under the skin of the survivors.
Organic shrapnel.

6.

I want to speak about loss.
About my father and the word we never found.
In a dream Satan told me he was a crow
and that the small intestine was so long
God hid it in the stomach.
Perhaps this is why the death of a father
brings new life. Communion,
water and wine. Amen.
But the death of our mothers is annihilation.
There is no particular reason to believe me.

7.

When has death ever been silent?
The watchword is not mute, the cry comes from the deep.
I want to go further, but I am afraid.
There are ways in which the memory of my prison
is nothing more than a scarf trailing from the hand of
a child leaning over the side of a pier, signalling
to gulls, and surf, and indifferent waves,

before being snatched by the wind.
And though I have tears, I am grateful too.
On the boardwalk the Jimmy Hendrix lookalike smiles.
This is no time for hemlock.

8.

Every creation myth begins with owning land, or wanting to.
And gods plant us where we are with the help of others
that cannot be named.
I have made a talisman of my hope.
It is the glimmer of light from a house lost in the woods.
I have a cousin who walks with a shuffle.
It was cruel to think she was slow.
It is simply what circumcision does to some women.
I am looking for the words to say this.
But I remain a man, you see.
The knife is firmly in my hand.

PILGRIMAGE

1.

Nothing as definite as prayer.
A hand cups a shadow.
A heart is laid bare, open as a flower.
Somewhere between care and cacophony
Los Angeles is alive.
The city tonight stands outside of everything.
We come to night.
We come to light.
The city is a liar.
May I find my way.
Los Angeles is a dream we cannot bear.
I think of streets black as any river, and beer.
Over loud music a woman calls to her lover.
There is no truth here.
The city is awash with lights.
Even this sacrifice will not save us.
I say *hibiscus* and mean innocence.
I say *guava* and mean childhood.
I say *mosquito netting* and I mean loss.
I say *father* and it means only that.
Happen that we all dream, but the sea is only sea.
Happen that we call upon God but it is only a breeze
ruffling a prayer book in a small church
where benches groan in the heat.
Outside a peacock will not be quiet.
There are so many ways I could undo the night
my father expired, if only I could
find the fastenings of time.
Here the green grass is green even with the abundance
of home, even with the weight of exile.
There is a tree in my father's backyard under which
my umbilical is buried. There is no metaphor here.

Bathing on a zinc sheet one night, I sliced my ankle
to bleed my umbilical again.
Look, there is a simple math to loss, to self, to aubergines.
I can sing my father's lineage back half a millennia
but here in Starbucks I struggle with Oprah
to find myself. Which is to say,
I could accept the labels before me,
but only a deeper cut will suffice.
I am not an American, though I want to be.
I am not a Nigerian even though I have the melancholy.
I am something deeper still.
For now, Igbo, is a place holder. Also sometimes,
Druid, on my mother's side. And a red passport.
People say, Christ, if I'd seen what you've seen.
Christ! Mercy! Jesus!
This is my cry too. I have seen, but I am still lost.
The fog will not part no matter how long I strike
my staff against stone.
There are slavers in my ancestry, slaves too.
Some nights I wake with the bitter of rusty chains
on my tongue, a whip in my hand.
Avatars come and go and come again.
There is only a map fading in the harsh sun.
Some may call me a pessimist but I am not.
There is nothing gained from loss.
I drink tea in the shade and believe in poetry.
I am zealot for optimism.

2.

Every river is Jordan for the faithful.
They came to the holy mountain by my college.
They climbed for days in their white robes.
They looked like a flock of egrets
resting in the heat and the green.
Can a new sky be born?

Nothing I tell you will slake your thirst.
But Pepsi at a baseball game comes close.
If I mourn for all the suffering in the world,
then I have only my ego to blame.
I mourn daily. How can I not?
Let there be love.
There are 20 strings in a Myanmar marionette.
There are 54 ethnic groups in Vietnam.
There are 250 ethnic groups in Nigeria.
There are 100 petals on a blossom of
a Japanese Kikuzakura cherry tree.
Diwali last for only five days.
Then the lights dim and we forget.

3.

In Siena the bells toll to mark the hour.
Outside birds sing. Also scooters whine.
In Nigeria they were ridden by insurance agents
in white shirts. Kids would scream "American Life Mutual"
as they kicked up dust in their whiney trail.
As they say in France, *C'est la vie*.
I am like a man climbing a mountain but taking in
none of the view.
I don't know what faith is but
I know this much –
I want to put my fingers in the wounds and swirl them around.
Thomas has nothing on me.
I was seduced as a boy by frankincense
and smoke
and altar lights
and Latin mass
and robes
and wafers and wine
and wooden pews dark with sweat

and confessionals musty with lies
and rosary beads worried for a vision,
then Buddha and the romance of Tibet.
If Zeno's paradox reveals anything it is not that
space and time can be divided into infinity infinitely,
but simply this:
that we can only approximate the object of our desire;
that we are always on a train travelling to happiness.
But what we do reach is coffee, biscotti and Bob on the iPod.
Alexandria, in Egypt, is both a city and a library –
hope and destination.
The world is often like this.
Some things look like blood, some
even taste like mud and rust.
They are not blood. They are not.

4.

And God stands in disdain as we supplicate.
If love is your nature you will find it.
The frayed carpet and plastic-covered chairs
were the stage for my aunt's faith.
Dipping harddough bread into milky sweet tea
she unleashed her anger at the world in prayer.
In another life she could have been a dancer.
In this one, she is a Christian.
In Zimbabwe, Mugabe betrays a people
who make excuses for him.
This is what it is to be a president in Africa.
FUCK YOU HIGH QUALITY – bathroom graffiti, Siena.
In Nazi Germany, a student resistance group called
White Rose. Who knew?
Their slogan: *Wir Schweigen Nicht*.
We too will not be silent.
In June and July 1994, OJ made the cover of Newsweek.

By the time the Rwandan genocide made the cover
in August, 1 million were dead. 4 million displaced.

5.

Let me know this too:
the sting of orange zest in my eyes.
And chocolate, decadent and truffled.
And dancing.
And milk fresh and bubbling from a goat.
And the wind holding me as I freefall from a plane.
And wonder at a goldfish's infinite curiosity.
And cats.
And dogs.
And a child's hand brushing my face.
And wings.
And still rain.
And still rain.

6.

The root of the word *salary* is sal. Salt.
To be paid in salt.
Salt is the weight, salt is the worth, salt is this body.
Say *pepper*, say *amen*.
Some people are necromancers –
they summon repeatedly the body of their pain.
Sometimes I am like that – dissecting the dead.
Sometimes I am merely a practitioner of nostalgia.
Like those heady Nigerian afternoons filled with munching
sugarcane, the molding of fufu for the dip
into stew, fingers fishing for morsels of delight,
the cold slake of coconut water fresh from a nut.
Good fiction is simply the capacity to remember
your life, and yet simultaneously realize

you are inventing every memory.
When I was a child,
South Africa was a story about men
so deep into the despair of a bottle,
dreams dark as the coal they worked.
When I was a child,
vampires lived behind the water tank, skirted
by the modesty of elegant green bamboo.
Now as a man, in the café in Siena, I declare:
Those fucking Germans, those fucking Germans!
So what is my excuse now?

7.

It is easy to forget the decadence of glass.
How some of us only find it in fragments.
The glass between us and the world
is often the measure of our wealth.
Looking out at the world through it
colours the hunger beyond.

8.

Growing up Emeka was albino:
How we feared his pink skin and red eyes.
How we loathed him.
To my shame, I never ate with him,
saying: I just ate –
and to my sister, under my breath:
he disgusts me.
She never told on me, but made me wait
while she ate with him
– same plate, no utensils –
her eyes never leaving mine.

9.

Courage is often invisible:
Old women who buy their own groceries.
Mothers who become shadows.
Women who speak and speak and are not heard
until a man says, of course, of course.
Children walking through minefields.
Palestinians who don't throw stones,
wanting only food and life for their children.
Palestinians who throw stones,
wanting only food and life for their children.
Israelis who eat in cafés.
People who feed the homeless.
People who don't feed the homeless,
but love their children well.
People who love people.
Who love animals.
Young people who will not be fettered.
Old people who will not die quietly.
Women who dance with wolves.
Women who care for the dying.
People who speak of rage and abuse.
People who suffer pain with a smile.
People who suffer pain loudly.
People who speak up for their beliefs.
Children who protect other children.
Homeless children who smile.
People who have to navigate worlds designed,
consciously or not, to keep them out.
Being Black anywhere in the 21st century.

10.

In Siena, in a beautiful café on Palazzo Del Campo
drinking coffee while Eastern European refugees beg,
a man says to me: Literature in Italy is not like Nigeria.

There is no suffering here. We have no problems to fight.
The clock on the tower says 4 p.m.
What can be said to a man listening to Bob Marley
on a train speeding through Tuscany?

11.

To see the Verrazzano Bridge disappear into fog
on a sunny Brooklyn day.

12.

Tonight I am waiting, alone,
in my hotel room. I am not waiting
for a lover, imagined or real.
I am waiting for my father.
Which is to say, my dead father.
What I want to understand is overwhelming.
The way a trap door in the floor holds nightmare.
I have lost all sense of scale.
The father I wait for is not real.
He is not the man who died five years ago.
And yet he cannot bend into metaphor.
I want to say I love him.
Barthes would say I do:
You do because you are waiting.
The way a plane cuts through clouds.
Like the Mandarin waiting for the courtesan for 99 days.
Like Blake setting a place for God.
Like the Red Vines I try to wrap around my rage.
The tender gesture says: Ask me anything.

BENEDICTION

1.

Let me tell you about sorrow.
A mother wandering down a street calling
for a child while planes scream overhead.
And bullets around her cutting down goats,
and trees and men and women and finally her,
and in the dust, just out of reach of her dead hand,
her son's severed head.
And somewhere, someone is wailing.
Let me tell you about hate.
A bayonet on the end of a rifle run through
a teenager's bony chest by a swarthy soldier
frothing from the pleasure of it, amazed
at the sound of it, flesh sucking on metal.
And this boy dying and
his eyes do not lose their burn,
staring at his killer as though to say,
Do it, do it now because I will do it to you
and even as I die, I am doing it to you.
Let me tell you about love.
Suheir on a rooftop in Jersey City cries into her cell.
They won't stop coming, she says.
Email after email after email.
And in them they are dying, or dead or afraid.
And I can't hold it, can't hold it.
We are talking about Lebanon and Gaza.
In Los Angeles I make soothing sounds,
as I fill the pot for coffee. I wonder
if I will still be able to watch *CSI*.

2.

A cubist way to see the world.
Fractured histories,
at once present and absent.
What is this stone tongue that won't let me
make poetry in Igbo?
Akwa – egg
Akwa – cloth
Akwa – cry
Akwa – bed
Tone is God.
Akwa kwara akwa maka na akwa ya kuwara na akwa.
the cloth cried because its egg broke
on the hardness of the bed.
This is not avant-garde. This is Igbo.
Ehagi bu egu nagu irem.
Your name is a hunger on my tongue.
Enya gi bu ihe na echekwubem.
Your eyes are the light that shelters me.
Omoloma gi but omoloma'm.
Your beauty makes me beautiful.
I bu ndu na edubem.
You are my reason for living.
These words I learned tell me nothing:
faith, god, fire, man, death, sun, wind,
sea, sea, sea.
I learned *dictator* and it meant empty.
I learned *fratricide*.
I learned to hate and the world ground on.
In a bleak time, those who indulge are sybarites.
I am choosing a name for my lover.
Nganga – elegance.
Amara – grace.
Ngozi – blessing.
In the old country my mother planted flowers

in the face of my father's disdain.
In every garden,
in every house,
no matter how long
we lived there.
I think it was the war,
the blitz in England, that took all the flowers.
I think it was for the love she couldn't show him.
I think it was for me.
To show me that only the unspeakable remains.
And remains as gesture.
Eden is not the thing we seek.
It is the thing we cannot find.
It hangs tremulous like a spider's web from a branch.
This is the body of Christ.
Amen

RENEWAL

1.

Water and sand and the world.
This was my childhood.
And rice steaming under tomato stew heavy with chicken and thyme.
And ice-cream melted and coarse to the taste.
And the endless cough of savannah.
And chopper bicycles.
I am speaking of Afikpo.
The slant of the telling and it means according to each man.
The gang or the police.
The bumper car or helicopter.
The killing or the clubbing.
Particular, like the scent of summer light.
I am speaking of Los Angeles.
Holy be the Crips.
Holy be the Bloods.
Holy be the 18th Street.
Holy be the LAPD.
The historical narrative hinges on the sound
of a car cutting the gravel as it turns.
The war is still raging.
The poor keep dying.
Which is to say, young Americans.
Which is to say, young Palestinians.
Which is to say, young Israelis.
Which is to say, young Africans.
It's not that the rich don't care,
but how can the Virgin be set free of the icon?
Marvin sang and sang, but the spell didn't work.
It's still happening, brother.
This is how we suppress the trauma.
The Turks are lying about the Armenian ghosts.
I want to rampage through the world and rectify:

Blood for blood.
Death for death.
What can happen to all this hate?
Where do I bury it?
To exit is the first stage of enlightenment.

2.

There are four mothers for the world.
For the joy of this knowledge.
The mother is lost.
Holy the mother.
Holy, holy, holy.
What have we built? As Igbos, what have we built?
Perhaps the greatest bridge to the waking world across dreams,
between what can be imagined and said.
But what use is this if we cannot buy rice?
What good is it if we squander it?
I will follow the Nile one day.
And the Niger too. Perhaps even the Cross.
Glory be to free-flowing water.
Soon it will be gone and sand
makes a less adequate metaphor,
shifting and erasing the tracks in it.
If I were really a philosopher I would travel.
My continent awaits me.
Africa is a dream for us all.

3.

Have you ever woken to find it *was* you
drinking coffee and looking out all along?
We killed our grandfathers.
Then we killed our fathers.
Now we are killing ourselves.

Next will be the sons.
This is our legacy.
For fear of being loved we will kill the world.
Sometimes a bird slicing sky has no other meaning.
Sometimes water slakes our thirst.
Even this can be enough.

4.

My mother left a question mark, an unresolved ellipsis,
an echo maybe of a robin fluttering between grey
gravestones rising like abrupt cliffs in the sea of green.
I am her desire spreading into night like a rude whisper.

Now there is little to mark my days
save the slow steady reliability of water,
and a pump that measures, in perfect cups,
the shallow depths of each falling away
into an endless bucket, like a door opening to shadow,
and the way her heart held it open for me.

5.

How foolish of me to keep knocking
on the door to a heart whose face remains closed to me.
All these words, Father, all these words written
searching for you when it was never you, was it?
It was always me.
If I could build you a funeral pyre
I would lay down my hairbrush,
my GI Joe,
my books,
my pencils,
my drawings,
my books,

my dreams,
my books,
all.
Then fire.
I set you free that night, father.
When you came back in that yellow Volkswagen,
in that dream.
I made a boat of honour for you.
Woven of poems and words and not words.
I set it on the ocean.
Fr. Obuna said to me,
a gift is freely given and a gift
is freely returned.
It has taken me thirty years
to understand this.
Yemaja has your heart now.
May she be merciful.
May she love you.
The wound bleeds no more.
Which is to say,
what I have desired is like salt
left out all night and gone.
Dew be soft.
Dew be salty.

6.

Bean.
I feel so alive in you.
Damn the dead.
Damn the dying.
This is a hard light to weave words in.
If men could truly write love letters,
what would we say?
Jesus forgive this stake.

I must drive it home.
Something must die, for us to live.
We still haven't figured out the way.
From the train window
a lone tree grows out of a pylon.

7.

I want to say this:
What is left after the poet's gaze rips into us?
Cadaver?
Body?
Light?
If butterflies could know this melancholy.
This is a terrible, tragic alchemy.
But I will work the metal of my being
until it reflects only what is there.
And can I stand before this pure id?
Before this darkness that can burn the cornea?
Which is to say that there is only light.
Which is to say that there are only angels.
Which is to say that this is not death.
Holy is the hope.
Holy is the desire.
Holy is the awe.
Holy, holy, holy.
Amen.

8.

This is not a lamentation, damn it.
This is a love song.
This is a love song.
Like reggae – it all falls on the off beat.

If there is a way, it is here.
They say you cannot say this in a poem.
That you cannot say *love* and mean anything.
That you cannot say *soul* and approach heaven.
But the sun is no fool, I tell you.
It will rise for nothing less.

ABOUT THE AUTHOR

Chris Abani's prose includes *Song For Night* (Akashic, 2007), *The Virgin of Flames* (Penguin, 2007), *Becoming Abigail* (Akashic, 2006), *GraceLand* (FSG, 2004), and *Masters of the Board* (Delta, 1985). His poetry collections are: *Sanctificum* (Copper Canyon Press, 2010),*There Are No Names for Red* (Red Hen Press, 2010), *Hands Washing Water* (Copper Canyon, 2006), *Dog Woman* (Red Hen, 2004), *Daphne's Lot* (Red Hen, 2003), and *Kalakuta Republic* (Saqi, 2001).

He is a Professor at the University of California, Riverside and the recipient of the PEN USA Freedom-to-Write Award, the Prince Claus Award, a Lannan Literary Fellowship, a California Book Award, a Hurston/Wright Legacy Award, a PEN Beyond the Margins Award, the PEN Hemingway Book Prize & a Guggenheim Award.

NEW POETRY FROM PEEPAL TREE

Christian Campbell
Running the Dusk
ISBN: 9781845231552; pp. 84, June 2010; £8.99

Christian Campbell takes us to dusk, what the French call *l'heure entre chien et loup*, the hour between dog and wolf, to explore ambiguity and intersection, danger and desire, loss and possibility. These poems of wild imagination shift shape and shift generation, remapping Caribbean, British and African American geographies: Oxford becomes Oxfraud; Shabba Ranks duets with Césaire; Sidney Poitier is reconsidered in an exam question; market women hawk poetry beside knock-off Gucci bags; elegies for ancestors are also for land and sea. Here is dancing at the crossroads between reverence and irreverence. Dusk is memory, dusk is dream, dusk is a way to re-imagine the past.

Kwame Dawes
Back of Mount Peace
ISBN: 9781845231248; pp. 96, February 2010; £8.99

A retired fisherman, Monty Cupidon, encounters a naked, bloodied and traumatised woman standing at the cross-roads. He offers comfort and takes her in. Suffering from amnesia, she cannot tell him anything about herself. The only clues are the signs that she has once worn a wedding ring, has a butterfly tattoo and red nail polish on her toes. In the absence of memory, he names her Esther. So begins a remarkable sequence of poems that explores many dimensions of liminality. *Back of Mount Peace* explores the space between body and mind, making Esther's halting discovery of her self through her body, which like a tree bears its indelible history, work both as moving narrative device and a deeply sensual reminder of the physicality of existence.

Above all, this is a sequence that explores a relationship which begins in a primal Edenic space of innocent discovery in which, as Monty hopes, 'the hallelujah's of new love will begin', but which, like all relationships must enter history, the decay of time and the corruptions of knowledge..

Ishion Hutchinson
Far District
ISBN: 9781845231576; pp. 96, April 2010; £8.99

Far District explores a journey between worlds: the familiar culture of the rural village, which the poet-speaker feels ambivalent towards, and the world of western learning, the "luminous sea of myth" that the writer has felt shut out of because of physical and intellectual poverty. As the poet's journey takes him away from home and into the world of books and learning, there comes a new vision of what "home" might offer – a vision that can be represented through memory and the literary imagination.

Far District is a marvellous book of generous, giving poems. Not only does this collection travel through an abiding language and far-reaching imagery, but it also transports the reader to a complex psychological terrain through a basic honesty and truthfulness. The leap-frogging of borders is executed with an ease that never fails to engage the reader's mind and body. There's a playfulness here that's contagious and, at times, even outrageous in its breathless insinuation through a biting clarity and directness that would have challenged The Great Sparrow. Hutchinson is a young poet who seems to journey wherever his poems take him, and the reader is blessed to accompany him.

– Yusef Komunyakaa

Contact us at:
Peepal Tree Press, 17 King's Avenue, Leeds LS6 1QS, UK
Tel: +44 (0) 113 2451703 E-mail: contact@peepaltreepress.com